Part-time Students and their Experience of Higher Education

TOM BOURNER
WITH ANDY REYNOLDS,
MAHMOUD HAMED AND
RONALD BARNETT

The Society for Research into Higher Education
& Open University Press

Published by SRHE and
Open University Press
Celtic Court
22 Ballmoor
Buckingham
MK18 1XW

and
1900 Frost Road, Suite 101
Bristol, PA 19007, USA

First published 1991

British Library Cataloguing in Publication Data

Bourner, Tom
  Part-time students and their experience of higher education. – (The Cutting edge)
  1. Great Britain. Higher education institutions. Students
  I. Title II. Society for Research into Higher Education
  378.1980941

  ISBN 0 335 09351 4
  ISBN 0 335 09350 7 pbk

Library of Congress Cataloging-in-Publication Data

Bourner, Tom, 1955–
  Part-time students and their experience of higher education / by Tom Bourner with
  Andy Reynolds, Mahmoud Hamed and Ronald Barnett.
      p. cm.
  Includes bibliographical references and index.
  ISBN 0-335-09351-5. – ISBN 0-335-09350-7 (pbk.)
    1. Students, Part-time – Great Britain. 2. College students – Great Britain.
  I. Reynolds, Andy, 1957– . II. Hamed, Mahmoud, 1952–
  III. Barnett, Ronald, 1947– . IV. Title.
  LA637.7.B65 1991
  378.1'98'0941–dc20
                                              90-45378 CIP

Typeset by Rowland Phototypesetting Ltd
Bury St Edmunds, Suffolk
Printed in Great Britain by
St Edmundsbury Press Ltd, Bury St Edmunds, Suffolk

Part-time Students, and their Experience of Higher Education

THE CUTTING EDGE

Series Editors:
Malcolm Tight, Senior Lecturer in Continuing Education, University of Warwick.
Susan Warner Weil, Associate Director of Higher Education for Capability, the RSA.

This series deals with critical issues and significant developments in continuing education, focusing on its impact on higher education.

Current titles in the series:

Tom Bourner *et al.*: *Part-Time Students and their Experience of Higher Education*
David Smith and Michael Saunders: *Other Routes: Part-Time Higher Education Policy*

Contents

List of Tables

Series Editor's Introduction

Part-time Students and their Experience of Higher Education is one of the first books to be published in a new Society for Research into Higher Education/Open University Press series, *The Cutting Edge*. This series seeks to address the critical issues, and report upon significant research and development activity, at the cutting edge of continuing higher education.

The Cutting Edge series is based on the premise that social, demographic, economic and technological trends are now combining to ensure that virtually all institutions of higher education are concerned to open up their provision to new kinds of students. It is highly appropriate that this book should be one of the first published in the series, therefore, since part-time provision has been one of the major – if not *the* major – growth areas of British higher education over the last two decades.

In this book, Tom Bourner and his collaborators from Brighton Polytechnic and the Council for National Academic Awards present a detailed analysis of the characteristics, motivations and experiences of part-time first degree students in British polytechnics and colleges in the mid-1980s. The data on which their analysis is based was collected through a questionnaire survey of nearly 3,000 students, and through a parallel survey of course leaders.

The analysis clearly demonstrates that part-time first degree students are a far from homogeneous group, and that their characteristics – demographic, educational, employment – are very different from those of conventional full-time students. Part-time students are, in short, much more *adult*.

Bourner and his colleagues go on to illustrate the varied mix of vocational and non-vocational aims held by part-time students on enrolment. They examine the significant barriers placed in the way of their enrolment, and look at the continuing problems – some of them arising from the conflicts of interest between study, work and domestic lives – faced by part-time students on course.

One chapter, by Ronald Barnett, considers the institutions' approaches to part-time degree provision, focusing in particular on their practices with regard to publicity, enrolment, teaching and support. Another chapter concentrates on the issue of student non-completion, and considers how it might best be tackled. The book concludes by summarizing examples of good practice in course development and presentation.

Bourner, Reynolds, Hamed and Barnett have provided in this book both a summary of existing circumstances and a practical guide to future development. Their analysis and suggestions should be of considerable interest and use to both new and established providers in this expanding area of higher education.

Part-time Students and their Experience of Higher Education can be read in conjunction with two other books recently published by the Society for Research into Higher Education/Open University Press. One of these – Other Routes: Part-time Higher Education Policy, by David Smith and Michael Saunders – has been published simultaneously in *The Cutting Edge* series. This examines the changing policy context within which part-time degrees are being developed, and provides a complementary analysis of the structure and funding of these courses. The second book – *Higher Education: A Part-Time Perspective*, by myself – was published last year. It offers a comprehensive analysis of the nature and value of all forms and levels of part-time higher education in the United Kingdom, placing it in a historical and comparative context.

Malcolm Tight

Preface

The part-time sector of higher education is a large and growing part of higher education. So far it has attracted comparatively little attention from researchers or from other writers on higher education. This is particularly true of part-time higher education outside of the Open University. Little is known about who are the part-time students or about their experience of higher education.

Most part-time undergraduates outside of the Open University are studying in the polytechnics and colleges of higher education. Consequently, this book focuses on the experiences of the students in that sector.

The fall in the numbers of school leavers into the 1990s is generating much interest within institutions of higher education in wider access in general and in the further development of part-time degree courses in particular. A sign of this growing interest was the funding by the Council for National Academic Awards (CNAA) of a research project that generated the information on which this book is based.

We would like to thank members of the project's steering committee for their support in completing the project. We would also like to offer a special thanks to Professor Peter Toyne, who chaired the steering committee, and Dr Philip Jones, who was our 'link person' with CNAA Development Services, for their encouragement throughout the project.

A major part of the project was a questionnaire survey. Copies of the questionnaire can be obtained from CNAA Development Services, 344–354 Gray's Inn Road, London WC1X 8PB, UK.

The aims of this book are:

1. To provide an account of *who part-time students are* in terms of age, sex, backgrounds, previous education, previous qualifications, sectors of employment, and so on.
2. To explain the reasons why students choose the courses of part-time study that they do. In particular, to explain why they choose on-site degree-level study when distance learning provision is available from the Open University.
3. To identify the nature of the difficulties encountered by part-time students.
4. To give an account of the extent and incidence of student drop-out from

part-time degree courses and to indicate factors that are systematically related to it.

5. To identify examples of 'good practice' in the provision and management of part-time degree courses.

This book addresses critical issues in the provision of part-time higher education. Our intention is that it will contribute to the dissemination of 'good practice' by widening awareness of the diversity of practices in the provision of part-time higher education. We hope that course teams will find in the book ideas from other part-time degree courses and from the experiences of students that will be helpful in developing and operating their own courses. More generally, we hope that it will be of value to all those who are promoting, developing, managing, teaching or studying on part-time courses of higher education.

Tom Bourner
Andy Reynolds
Mahmoud Hamed
Ronald Barnett

Note to the Reader

The following points should be borne in mind when reading the tables in this book:

1. The percentages have been rounded up to one decimal place or to the nearest whole number. Consequently, some columns (or rows) do not sum to exactly 100 per cent.
2. Where figures have been rounded to one decimal place, 0.55 or more has been rounded to 0.6. Where figures have been rounded to the nearest whole number, 0.5 has been rounded to 1.
3. Respondents for whom there is no information on a given variable have been excluded from the analysis.

List of Abbreviations

Various abbreviations have been used in this report. Normally, the first occurrence has been placed in parentheses following the full text. The abbreviations used are as follows:

ACID Association of Colleges Implementing DipHE programmes
AFE   Advanced Further Education
BTEC Business and Technician Education Council
CNAA Council for National Academic Awards
DES   Department of Education and Science
DipHE Diploma in Higher Education
FESR Further Education Statistical Record
FT   Full-time
FTE   Full-time Equivalent
HNC   Higher National Certificate
HND   Higher National Diploma
LEA   Local Education Authority
NAB   National Advisory Body
NEDC National Economic Development Council
NUS   National Union of Students
ONC   Ordinary National Certificate
OND   Ordinary National Diploma
OU   Open University
PCAS Polytechnics Central Admissions Service
PCFC Polytechnics and Colleges Funding Council
PSHE Public Sector of Higher Education
SW   Sandwich
UGC   University Grants Committee
USR   Universities Statistical Record
WEA   Workers' Educational Authority

1 | The Provision of Part-time Degree Courses

Introduction

Compared to full-time higher education, the information available on part-time higher education is very limited. This is illustrated, for example, by the fact that the Department of Education and Science (DES) collects data on the degree performance of full-time and sandwich students but not on those who complete part-time courses of higher education. This neglect in official statistics is mirrored in the relative paucity of research literature on mature students generally, and on part-time students in particular, in public sector higher education.

After surveying the research literature on mature students in British higher education, Alan Woodley concluded that compared to the Open University and conventional universities very little work has been done in polytechnics and colleges of higher education (see Piper, 1982, p. 81). Recently, however, interest in continuing education has increased substantially on both sides of the higher education binary line, as evidenced by major reports on continuing education by both the National Advisory Body (NAB) and the University Grants Committee (UGC) in 1984.

The segments of higher education described by the terms 'mature students', 'continuing education' and 'part-time provision' are by no means synonymous. The overlap, however, is considerable, and may be illustrated by Fig. 1.1. Some mature students are enrolled on full-time or sandwich courses and some of the students enrolled on these courses are engaged in a process of continuing education. However, all part-time students are engaged in continuing education and they are all, or nearly all, mature – depending on the precise definition of 'maturity'. Quantitatively, part-time students comprise the large majority of mature students in continuing education. They may reasonably be regarded as the kernel of both the 'mature student' and 'continuing education' categories.

Advocacy of the importance of part-time provision has been a recurring theme in statements on the role of the non-university sector of higher education since the 1960s. For example:

All advanced further education

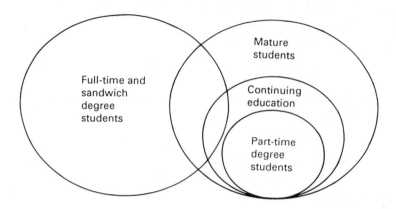

Figure 1.1   The components of higher education.

The academic range of the polytechnic should clearly be determined by the needs of part-time students rather than those of full-time students, for the part-time students have nowhere else to go. (Robinson, 1968)

Part-time courses should not be regarded as cheap and nasty alternatives to full-time education, nor as a sop to the mature student, nor as a means of providing cheap labour. I hold that the part-time route is not only valuable but essential, that it can, with proper and effective organisation, offer a worthwhile educational experience and that we should be seeking dignity not denigration in part-time provision. (Tolley, 1975)

It is one of the special tasks of public sector higher education to explore the limits of access and to see how far it is possible to extend opportunities without sacrificing the quality of the education offered while maintaining the provision of personal and social and economic benefits. . . . The higher education system of the future, however, whatever its size and shape, must also provide for dispersed access. Not all students are mobile. Mature students and part-time students typically need access to local institutions: and it is probably true that the non-traditional entrant is often more readily attracted to a local college than to a more distant institution. If we are serious about the extension of access, we must provide a system that meets the needs of such students. (Ball, 1985, p. 74)

Despite its acknowledged importance, knowledge about part-time provision in the public sector of higher education remains very limited. The research project on which this book is based was designed to provide such knowledge. It focuses on the part-time students (rather than on the courses or on the institutional settings), as this is the area where the available information is most limited.

Part-time students in the public sector of higher education

Relative size of part-time provision

Over the last decade, part-time student enrolments in higher education have grown at more than three times the rate of that of full-time students (Table 1.1) In 1975, part-time students accounted for less than 30 per cent of all those enrolled on course of higher education. If current trends continue, at some time in the 1990s the part-timers will constitute a *majority* of those in higher education.

Table 1.1   Part-time and full-time students in higher education in the UK, 1975–87 (thousands).

| | 1975 | | 1987 | | % change |
	No.	%	No.	%	1975–87
Part-time	215.1	(29.9)	359.3	(37.1)	+67
Full-time[a]	503.8	(70.1)	608.7	(62.9)	+21
Total	718.9	(100)	968.0	(100)	

Source: Department of Education and Science (1989, table 1).
[a] Includes sandwich courses.

Growth of part-time higher education by sector of higher education

Although the provision of higher education to part-time students has expanded greatly since the mid-1970s, different sectors of higher education have experienced different rates of growth (Table 1.2). Each of the sectors of higher

Table 1.2   Part-time students in higher education in the UK by sector, 1975–87 (thousands).

| | 1975 | | 1987 | | % change |
	No.	%	No.	%	1975–87
Polytechnics and colleges	134.1	(62.3)	232.7	(64.8)	+74
Open University	56.0	(26.0)	85.8	(23.9)	+53
Other universities	25.0	(11.6)	40.7	(11.3)	+63
Total	215.1	(100)	359.2	(100)	

Source: Department of Education and Science (1989, table 1).

education has shared in the boom in part-time students. It is interesting to observe, however, that the growth has been slower in the Open University – which for some people is synonymous with part-time higher education – than in the polytechnics, other colleges and the other universities.

Undergraduate provision compared with other part-time provision

It may be surprising to some that there is more sub-degree part-time work undertaken in institutions of higher education in the UK than work at first degree level or above. Most of this work is undertaken outside of the universities in the polytechnics and colleges of higher education (Table 1.3). It is interesting to observe, however, that part-time sub-degree work is expanding less rapidly than part-time degree and postgraduate work.

The study on which this book is based concentrated on students on first degree courses. We felt that it was better to focus on one of the major segments of part-time provision that is fairly homogeneous, rather than attempt to cover a wider range of provision more superficially.

Sources of information

The sources of information were, at the outset of the project, expected to be Council for National Academic Awards (CNAA) records, DES records and Open University records, supplemented by a questionnaire study of students currently enrolled on CNAA part-time first degree courses. It soon became apparent that the paucity of existing records on part-time students in higher education meant that greater reliance than expected would have to be placed on primary data collection. For this purpose, the main vehicle was a large-scale questionnaire survey of part-time undergraduates.

Table 1.3   Part-time students in higher education in the UK by level of course, 1975–87 (thousands).

	1975		*1987*		*% change*
	No.	*%*	*No.*	*%*	*1975–87*
Part-time postgraduate	30.1	(14.0)	55.8	(15.5)	+85
Part-time undergraduate	59.8	(27.8)	101.7	(28.3)	+70
Part-time sub-degree	125.2	(58.2)	201.8	(56.2)	+61
Total	215.1	(100)	359.3	(100)	

Source: Department of Education and Science (1989, table 1).

The student questionnaire

Questionnaire design

The student questionnaire was highly structured in the sense that almost all of the questions were pre-coded. This approach economizes on resources at the data preparation stage but is resource-intensive at the questionnaire design stage. This, in turn, makes the piloting stage particularly important as respondents were likely to abandon the questionnaire if the range of pre-coded answers was too limited or inappropriate. Hence, unless the questionnaire was well-constructed, the response rate would probably be low.

The questions included in the first draft of the questionnaire were, of course, based primarily on the objectives of the study. There were, however, other influencing factors. First, questions were drawn from related questionnaire studies. These provided some questions that had been tested in the field and also established standards for comparability. For the most part, the temptation to 'improve' on the wording of questions that had been used in previous questionnaires was resisted on the grounds that the opportunity for comparability would thereby be lost. Sometimes, however, this temptation proved too strong.

A major source of questions was the questionnaire used by the 'Mature Students' enquiry undertaken for the DES by a consortium of education researchers from the Open University, the Polytechnic of Central London and Lancaster University (see Fulton *et al.*, 1987). Secondly, it was decided to give more attention to the courses (in addition to the students) than would seem justified from the original objectives of the project. The reasons for this followed from a belief that an important aim of the project should be to help course leaders and course teams improve course provision even if this should mean some widening of the declared objectives of the project. This may be seen as a decision to give the project more of a policy orientation than was present in the original project proposal. This approach can also be explained in terms of the project's original objectives, however, by relating the wide range of course-orientated questions in the questionnaire to the issue of student wastage. Finally, it was felt that both course leaders and students would be more prepared to cooperate with the survey if course improvements were clearly seen to be a likely result of the project.

The questionnaire went through numerous drafts. Various versions were sent for comment to people with special interests in, or experience of, part-time higher education. These people were extremely generous with their time and the comments received resulted in many changes to the original draft. Further drafts of the questionnaire were piloted with groups of part-time students at Brighton Polytechnic and at Birmingham Polytechnic. Finally, the penultimate version was administered (in the presence of the project leader) to students enrolled on a part-time Business Studies degree at Brighton Polytechnic.

Sampling strategy

An analysis of the distribution of student numbers enrolled on CNAA part-time degree courses showed that 16 subject areas each had at least five courses in operation and that these 16 subject areas accounted for over 80 per cent of the students. The subjects that were included in the analysis are as follows:

- art and design (including photography),
- humanities,
- social sciences,
- law,
- education,
- biological sciences,
- chemistry,
- computer studies,
- mathematics,
- physics,
- electrical/electronic engineering,
- mechanical engineering,
- other engineering (not elsewhere specified),
- materials studies,
- quantity surveying, and
- business studies.

The possibility of sampling a limited number of students from all of the courses was considered, but rejected for two reasons: first, concentration on a limited number of courses would permit the use of course prospectus material as a supplementary resource to aid analysis and interpretation of the questionnaire returns; and secondly, there were practical problems with the alternative approach – either all course leaders could be asked for the names and addresses of all of the students to permit random sampling by the project officers or course leaders could be asked to undertake the sampling and send to the project team only the names and addresses of those selected. Both approaches would have placed a heavy burden on hard-pressed course leaders – and we have grounds for thinking that course leadership of part-time courses can be particularly onerous. Also, it was felt that the responsibility for sample selection should remain with the researchers.

Instead, therefore, we decided to sample all students on sufficient courses to encompass approximately 25 per cent of the above students. It was decided to exceed the 25 per cent criterion in those subjects with small numbers of students (e.g. art and design) to produce a sample large enough to produce statistically meaningful results. Similar considerations led to less than 25 per cent of the students being contacted in those subjects (e.g. education) with large numbers of part-time students.

Initially, courses in each subject area were randomly selected until the 'approximately 25 per cent' criterion was met. Subsequently, some small adjustments of the sample were made to ensure that as far as possible there was some representation of the following within each of the subject areas:

1. Both polytechnic and other public sector colleges.
2. Both honours and non-honours courses.
3. Recently approved courses and well-established courses.

Most of the objectives of the project are student-orientated and the remainder are institution- or course-orientated. It would have been desirable to stratify the sample along all significant dimensions of student and course and institution type. This would have allowed minimization of the overall sample size necessary to obtain an adequate number of respondents within each student and/or course category for meaningful statistical analysis. The main problems with this approach were:

1. We were not in a position to stratify according to student characteristics, as the balance of student characteristics in the population of CNAA undergraduates was not known – this indeed was what the survey was designed to find out.
2. The meaningful dimensions along which it was possible to stratify by course/college were numerous. They inculde:

   - course balance (including, for example, honours and non-honours balance, duration of course, available modes of attendance, etc.),
   - subject balance (including, for example, subject area, number of courses per subject and number of students per course),
   - institutional balance (including, for example, ratio of full-time to sandwich students within colleges), and
   - regional balance.

To have stratified the sample along all of these dimensions, for which there are data on a national basis, would have been possible but the justification for so doing was not clear as we did not have well-framed hypotheses about how these factors affected the student profiles or the nature of the courses/colleges. For this reason, it was decided to adopt the (almost) random sampling strategy explained above.

About 26 per cent of the students in 16 subject areas were sent questionnaires in 1985. This represented 21.5 per cent of the total of 15 391 part-time CNAA undergraduates enrolled on all subjects at that time.

Response rate
The final version of the questionnaire was distributed to 4227 part-time undergraduates in 1985. The sample population comprised all of the students enrolled on 66 part-time degree courses approved by the CNAA. A reminder was distributed to those who had not responded. A total of 52 questionnaires were returned 'address unknown' (or similar), so that to the best of our knowledge 4175 questionnaires reached their destinations. Altogether, 2876 usable completed questionnaires were returned, giving an overall response rate of almost 70 per cent. This was a high response rate for such a long and detailed questionnaire (even after photo-reduction, the questionnaire ran to 18 pages and the pilot studies had indicated that it took about one hour to complete). It is

a tribute to the respondents that they should have been willing to give up so much of their time for the prospect of improvements in part-time provision that might benefit not themselves but *future* generations of students.

The level of response may be compared with a previous attempt at a national survey of part-time students (Whitburn *et al.*, 1976), where a response rate of 40 per cent was obtained. It may also be compared with the 50 per cent response rate obtained from the more recent national questionnaire survey of mature students on qualifying courses undertaken for the DES (Fulton *et al.*, 1987). In the latter study, it was noted that:

> . . . we [*sic*] achieved better response rates from mature students taking high- rather than low-level courses, from those studying full-time rather than part-time, and from those taking cognitive and intellectual courses rather than practical and leisure-type courses. (p. 35)

The response rate for none of the subjects fell below 60 per cent, with quantity surveying the lowest at 61 per cent. At the other end of the range, the response rate for mechanical engineering was 84 per cent (Table 1.4).

Distribution of responses by type of course
Almost half of the respondents were enrolled on courses that permitted students to complete either an honours degree or a non-honours degree. Of the remainder, rather more of the students (27 per cent) were enrolled on honours courses than on non-honours courses (23 per cent).

The most common pattern of attendance is evening only (accounting for over 45 per cent of the respondents). The next most common pattern is one day plus

Table 1.4   Response rates by subject.

Subject	%
Mechanical engineering	84
Metallurgy/materials sciences	80
Engineering*	76
Education	72
Humanities	71
Electrical/electronic engineering	70
Physics	70
Mathematics	68
Biological sciences	66
Chemistry	66
Computer studies	66
Art and design (including photography)	65
Social sciences	68
Business studies	63
Law	63
Quantity surveying	61
All subjects combined	69

* Not elsewhere specified

Table 1.5   The courses in the survey.

Empty first year	2
Empty second year	3
Short (less than 3 years)	10
Immature (i.e. recently approved)[a]	16
The rest	35
Total	66

[a] Students not yet enrolled on final stage.

evening/s (26 per cent) followed by half-day plus evening/s (13 per cent). Other patterns of attendance are comparatively rare.

Not all of the courses recruit students each year and, of course, not all are of the same length. Some courses are relatively short, being specifically designed to 'top up' other advanced further education (AFE) courses such as Higher National Certificate (HNC) or a teaching qualification. Finally, some courses are still 'immature' in the sense that they are sufficiently recently approved that they do not yet have students who have reached the final stage. Table 1.5 gives a breakdown of the courses in the survey.

Almost one-quarter of the students had been exempted from some part of their degree course. The majority of these exemptions are accounted for by the 10 courses designed to 'top up' other AFE courses. On other courses, exemptions are comparatively rare.

Distribution of respondents by year and subject

Most of the respondents were in the first or second year of enrolment on their degree courses (Table 1.6). The preponderance of first- and second-year students is partly a reflection of the fact that some courses are relatively 'young', i.e. they had been approved too recently to have students enrolled on all years of the course; partly a reflection of non-completion by students; partly a reflection of the fact that some of the courses do not recruit each year; and partly a reflection of the fact that some courses are of short duration (3 years or less), being designed to 'top up' other AFE courses such as HNC. The last two factors produced the distribution of responses to the question about 'normal' course

Table 1.6   Years of enrolment to date on course (including current year of enrolment).

Years	%
1	36
2	27
3	23
4 or more	14
Total	100

Table 1.7   Normal duration
(in years) for completion of
course as a part-time student.

Years	%
3 or less	19
4	40
5 or more	41
Total	100

duration shown in Table 1.7. In terms of years 'remaining to completion of the course', the respondents were more evenly distributed (Table 1.8).

Other data used

In addition to the results of the students' questionnaire, we also drew information from a more unstructured questionnaire sent to the 66 course leaders of the courses included in the students' questionnaire survey. The questions on the course leaders' questionnaire were much more open-ended than those on the student questionnaire. This was because the nature of the information sought was necessarily less structured and therefore less susceptible to pre-coding. Indeed, an important objective of this part of the exercise was to identify the *diversity* of the provision of facilities for part-time students. Secondary sources on information included records from within the CNAA, data from the DES Further Education Statistical Record and Open University statistics.

The investigation of student wastage presented a problem. Neither the DES nor the CNAA records permitted an effective analysis of the structure of student wastage of part-time undergraduates. Nor could the issue be adequately addressed by a simple questionnaire survey, as wastage is a dynamic process that is not easily captured by the snapshot approach of the survey method. It was clear, however, that this is a most important issue for those involved in the management of the courses and, of course, for the part-time students themselves.

Table 1.8   Expected years
remaining to completion of
course.

Years	%
1 or less	20
2	20
3	27
4 or more	33
Total	100

Our solution was to include questions in the student questionnaire that previous research suggested might be important to this issue, with the prospect of recontacting the respondents to discover those who had withdrawn without completion. We obtained information on the subsequent progress of all the students in the survey one year after the original enquiry. By linking the results of the 'recontacting' exercise to the datafiles, we were able to analyse the structure of student wastage and identify student and course characteristics that are systematically related to student wastage.

First, we conducted a follow-up survey one year after the original study and obtained a 70 per cent response rate. Only a small proportion of the responders were non-completers. We had a strong feeling that the non-completers were disproportionately heavily represented among the 30 per cent who had not responded. If this was the case, it would clearly seriously affect the validity and usefulness of the exercise.

Personalized reminder letters did not contribute much to the response rate and we decided to telephone the non-responders to identify their progress in the year since the main questionnaire had been distributed. This tactic did not prove successful and we abandoned it in favour of contacting the course leaders instead. This was much more successful and, eventually, we obtained information on the subsequent progress of *all* of the 2876 students who had completed the original questionnaire form.

2 | The Students: An Overview

This chapter looks at some of the characteristics of part-time degree students. It presents facts and figures on a range of parameters that show what kinds of people undertake part-time degree courses. There is no attempt to describe the 'typical part-time undergraduate', as the variation is often as revealing as the similarities. The chapter looks at demographic factors, socio-economic factors, previous education and qualifications and, finally, makes some comparisons with Open University students.

Demographic factors

Age

The average (median) age of respondents to the main questionnaire was 30. Almost 50 per cent of the students were between 25 and 35 years of age (Table 2.1). It might be expected that students on more vocationally orientated courses would tend to be younger than those on less vocationally orientated courses, as

Table 2.1 Age of CNAA part-time undergraduates.

Age	%
Under 20	1
20–24	21
25–29	26
30–34	19
35–39	16
40–49	14
51–59	3
60 and over	1
Total	101

Note: Mean = 32.

Table 2.2   Percentages of students aged under 30 by subject.

Subject	%
Quantity surveying	93
Chemistry	92
Biological sciences	83
Physics	82
Metallurgy/materials studies	82
Electrical/electronic engineering	70
Engineering*	66
Mechanical engineering	66
Computer studies	52
Business studies	51
Mathematics	35
Law	31
Art/design (including photography)	27
Social sciences	27
Education	11
Humanities	11
All subjects combined	47

* Not elsewhere specified

the 'present value of future income' generated by acquiring degree level qualifications tends to fall with increasing age. Table 2.2 suggests that the issue is rather more complicated. The presence of education, law and business studies in the bottom half of the table emphasizes the role of part-time higher education in *continuing* education in the fullest sense of the term.

Gender

Almost two-thirds of the respondents were male. Table 2.3 shows the variation across subjects. On part-time degree courses, the ratio of males to females (65:35) was higher than for full-time degree courses (55:45). However, this is, for the most part, the result of differences in the distribution of student numbers across subjects. On a subject-for-subject basis, the percentages of the students who were male on part-time courses were similar to those on full-time courses.

Marital status and domestic responsibilities

Most (60 per cent) of the part-time undergraduates were married. Being married can, of course, be a source of support for part-time students, but it can also be a source of other domestic commitments. This issue is investigated later in the book. As background, however, the following results from the survey are relevant:

Table 2.3   Gender of part-time undergraduates.

Subject	Male %	Female %
Engineering*	99	1
Mechanical engineering	98	2
Electrical/electronic engineering	97	3
Metallurgy/materials studies	96	4
Quantity surveying	95	5
Physics	92	8
Chemistry	79	31
Computer studies	75	25
Mathematics	69	31
Business studies	67	33
Law	61	39
Art/visual studies	59	41
Education	46	54
Biological sciences	39	61
Social studies	38	62
Humanities	29	71

* Not elsewhere specified

- Over 40 per cent of the respondents had children.
- Of those who were married, the spouse was in employment (full-time or part-time) in over 75 per cent of the cases.

Ethnic monitoring

Part-time degrees are sometimes believed to provide increased access to higher education to groups under-represented in the full-time student body. For this reason, the questionnaire asked about ethnic origin (Table 2.4). There is little evidence in these findings to suggest that part-time degrees in total are making a substantial contribution to the erosion of any educational disadvantage of those whose ethnic origins are not European/UK European. This does not imply, of course, that there are not some courses which are exceptions to this general finding. Our results are perhaps not too surprising in the light of results presented later in this chapter on the entry qualifications of part-time students. It may be that greater progress in this area depends upon more widespread availability of access courses.

Socio-economic monitoring

Employment status

A study of Open University students by Turnstall (1974) found that when occupation is considered, Open University students had already moved upward

Table 2.4 Ethnic origin of part-time undergraduates.

Origin	%
European/UK European	92
Asian/UK Asian	4
Caribbean/UK Caribbean	2
African/UK African	2
Other	0[a]
Total	100

[a] Less than 0.5 per cent.

in terms of their socio-economic status by the time that they enrolled for their Open University courses. The results of the enquiry into part-time students appear to tell a similar story. The percentages in Table 2.5 were computed from those to whom the question was applicable (so, for example, unmarried students were excluded before computing the last column). Compared with their parents, few of the respondents were engaged in manual occupations.

The data for the part-time students were not confined to those who were newly enrolled, and therefore it is difficult to assess any contribution that their degree studies had already made to their upward socio-economic mobility. The data is consistent with a story in which taking a part-time degree is part of the process of continued upward mobility.

Most of the respondents reported that both their parents left school at the age of 15 (Table 2.6). Taken together, Tables 2.5 and 2.6 suggest a pattern of

Table 2.5 Employment status of part-time students.

	Current or most recent employment (%)	First full-time employment after school (%)	Father[a] (%)	Mother[a] (%)	Spouse[c] (%)
Non-manual					
Professional[b]	46	23	17	11	36
Manager/employer	15	4	23	8	11
Other non-manual	31	46	15	38	35
Manual					
Skilled manual	7	16	25	9	11
Semi-skilled manual	1	5	12	11	4
Unskilled manual	1	7	8	22	3
Total[c]	101	101	100	99	100

[a] At the time that the respondent left school.
[b] Normally requiring qualifications of degree standard.
[c] Excludes those to whom the question was inapplicable.

Table 2.6   Age at which parents and spouse/partner left initial full-time education.

	Father (%)	Mother (%)	Spouse[a] (%)
16 or younger	82	85	45
17–18	8	9	27
19–22	6	5	21
Over 22	4	1	7
Total	100	100	100

[a] Where applicable.

intergenerational upward socio-economic mobility. In other words, the students enrolled on part-time first degree courses were continuing the process of upward social mobility of their parents.

The survey contributed another piece of information that is relevant to this issue. The questionnaire asked about any part-time study undertaken by parents or spouse/partner (where applicable). Of those who were able to give a definite answer to this question, the proportions who answered affirmatively were 33 per cent for father, 20 per cent for mother and 53 per cent for spouse/partner. These findings are consistent with a picture in which a significant proportion of the part-time students are in families in which continuing education is perceived to be associated with enhanced life chances.

Employment and jobs

About 90 per cent of the part-time undergraduates were in paid employment. Table 2.7 shows the figures for the respondents to the questionnaire. Professional and domestic commitments are likely to have a significant impact on the studies of undergraduates in paid employment. This is an issue which is picked up and explored later in the book.

For those in paid employment, the public sector accounts for a disproportionately large share cf the respondents. There appears to be evidence here to support the current disquiet that private industry has placed insufficient

Table 2.7   Employment status.

Status	%
Paid employment	89
Full-time housewife/person	4
Unemployed and seeking work	4
Self-employed	3
Unemployed and not seeking work	1
Other	1
Total	100

Table 2.8   Sector of employment.

Sector	%
Public sector	52
Private sector, manufacturing	25
Private sector, services	20
Other (e.g. voluntary agency)	3
Total	100

emphasis on continuing education and training (Table 2.8). Among those employed in the private sector, manufacturing accounts for a disproportionately large share of students.

It is interesting to compare total employment in UK manufacturing and services (Table 2.9) with Table 2.8. With service sector employment accounting for about three times that of manufacturing employment for the economy as a whole, the relatively small proportion of respondents employed in the service sector is notable. Perhaps the reason for this is that a large proportion of the polytechnics and other colleges have traditionally had closer links with manufacturing industry – arising from their origins in technical colleges and institutes of technology – and the current situation reflects these roots. If so, then the private service sector represents relatively unexplored territory for publicising part-time degree courses. With the continued decline of the manufacturing sector, it would seem to be important that this opportunity should not be neglected.

The respondents in paid employment are disproportionately represented among larger firms (Table 2.10). The relative concentration of part-time students within large organizations may reflect the fact that larger organizations place more weight on educational qualifications in career advancement or are more supportive of continuing education than smaller organizations. Another explanation might be that part-time courses direct their course publicity information at the more visible (larger) organizations. If the latter is the case, then course teams might consider whether greater awareness of part-time degree opportunities within smaller organizations would be worth pursuing.

Table 2.9   Employment in UK manufacturing and services (millions).

	1974	*1984*	% *change* *1974–84*
Manufacturing	8.9	5.6	−36.9
Services	13.6	15.1	+11.0

Source: NEDC (1984, p. 2).

Table 2.10   Employment of part-time undergraduates by size of organization.

No. of employees	% of respondents
10 or less	9
11–24	11
25–100	21
More than 100	60
Total	101

Work histories

Most of the respondents reported records of employment stability. Most had been with their current employer for at least 5 years. It should be recalled at this point that the median age of the respondents was 30 years. The distribution across the sample is shown in Table 2.11.

Only 9 per cent of the respondents had changed their job (employer) more than once in the 5 years before starting their part-time degree course; less than 10 per cent had changed their employer since starting their course. In reflecting on this high level of employment stability, it should be borne in mind that the 5 years up to the time of the survey was a period of high and rising national unemployment. A total of 80 per cent of the respondents reported that they had experienced no unemployment in the 5 years before starting their course and a further 15 per cent had experienced only one spell of unemployment. Over 90 per cent of the respondents reported that they had experienced no unemployment *since* starting their course, with only 1 per cent recording more than one spell of unemployment. The relatively low incidence of unemployment among those on part-time degree courses may be further evidence that such students are typically in relatively secure employment environments. Alternatively, it may mean that unemployment is so disruptive of part-time advanced level

Table 2.11   Number of years completed with current employer[a].

Years	%
0	9
1–2	14
3–5	28
6–10	32
11–20	15
Over 20	2
Total	100

[a] Applies only to those in current paid employment.

studies, that most of those who experienced unemployment had left their courses and were thereby excluded from the survey.

Membership of professional bodies

The survey sought information on the membership of professional bodies. The reason for including this question was to obtain information for course leaders who wish to explore whether professional bodies could provide an effective medium for publicizing their part-time degree courses. Most professional bodies have an interest in education and they offer a possible cost-effective medium through which to make contact with potential students. In particular, it is possible that professional bodies might be willing to include information on the availability of part-time degree courses that are relevant to their members via newsletters and the other ways by which they communicate with their members.

Overall, 31 per cent of the respondents reported that they were members of a professional body or institute. The results for individual subjects are shown in Table 2.12.

Apart from publicity resulting from announcements/mentions in newsletters, course leaders in particular subjects might consider combining together to support display advertisements in the journals of the relevant professional bodies. Thus, for example, the course leaders of part-time degree courses in mechanical engineering could jointly place an advertisement listing relevant

Table 2.12   Membership of professional bodies by individual subjects.

Subject	%
Metallurgy/materials studies	59
Education	56
Quantity surveying	37
Mechanical engineering	36
Law	35
Art/design (including photography)	32
Electrical/electronic engineering	29
Social sciences	29
Engineering*	26
Computer studies	26
Humanities	25
Business studies	23
Mathematics	21
Chemistry	16
Biological sciences	15
Physics	7
Total for all subjects	31

* Not elsewhere specified

Table 2.13   Type of school attended at age 14.

Type of school	%
Grammar	35
Comprehensive	26
Secondary modern	21
Independent	8
Overseas	5
Technical/commercial	3
Elementary	1
Total	99

part-time degree courses in the appropriate journal of the Institute of Mechanical Engineers.

Previous Education

Table 2.13 shows the type of school attended by the respondents at the age of 14. Those who had been to grammar schools formed the largest group (35 per cent), followed by those from comprehensives (26 per cent). Obviously, changes in the structure of secondary education would produce differences between the age groups in the sample. For the purposes of comparison, Table 2.14 compares the secondary education of respondents to the survey aged 25–30 with all school leavers in 1971–2 and also with entrants to full-time degree courses at polytechnics and colleges in 1974.

Table 2.14   Type of secondary school attended by CNAA part-time undergraduates aged 25–30, all school leavers 1971–2 and entrants to full-time polytechnic courses in 1974.

	CNAA part-time undergraduates aged 25–30 (%)	All school leavers, 1971–2[a] (%)	Entrants to full-time polytechnic courses, 1974[b] (%)
Secondary modern	19	37	17
Comprehensive[c]	36	42	14
State grammar	31	15	42
Independent and direct grant	7	8	18
Other	7	—	7
Total	100	100	98

[a] DES *Statistics of Education*, Vol. 4. (1974).
[b] Whitburn *et al.* (1976).
[c] Includes technical.

Table 2.15 School leaving age.

Age	%
16 or younger	47
17	16
18	33
19 or over	4
Total	100

The overall impression conveyed by Table 2.14 is of greater similarity between the type of secondary school attended by school leavers as a whole and part-time undergraduates, than students attending full-time higher education courses at polytechnics and colleges.

Leaving full-time education

The majority of the respondents left school at the age of 17 or younger. Indeed, almost half left school at the age of 16 or younger (Table 2.15). This pattern in the distribution of school leaving age is reflected in the qualifications obtained at school by the respondents (Table 2.16). It is clear that at the time of leaving school the large majority of the respondents would not have been in a position to meet the normal entry requirements for a degree course. However, many of those who left school at an early age proceeded to some other course of full-time study. Table 2.17 shows that a sizeable 38 per cent of the respondents had completed their initial full-time education at the age of 17 or younger. Many of those who develop part-time degree courses harbour hopes of providing a second chance of higher education for those who withdrew, or who were withdrawn, from education before having the opportunity to obtain the 'normal

Table 2.16 Highest level of qualification attained while at school.

Qualification	%
GCE 'A' level (two or more subjects) or Higher School Certificate	30
GCE 'A' level (one subject)	9
GCE 'O' levels (or CSE grade 1)	45
Qualifications below GCE 'O' level (including none)	11
Other	5
Total	100

Table 2.17   Age at which
full-time study was completed.

Age	%
16 or younger	27
17	11
18	21
19	7
20	7
21	14
Over 21	12
Total	99

minimum entry qualifications' for a degree course. According to Table 2.17, there is substance to these hopes.

Post-initial full-time education

Apart from those who proceeded *directly* to some other form of full-time study on leaving school, another sizeable group reported that they had subsequently undertaken some form of full-time study. Together, these two groups comprised 47 per cent of the respondents. For many this had not been a very satisfactory experience. Indeed, 18 per cent of the respondents had started but not finished such courses. There is evidence here that part-time degree courses are providing a 'second chance' for higher education.

For many part-time undergraduates, the gap between their last full-time study and their part-time degree course is substantial (Table 2.18). The average (median) period since the respondents were last engaged in full-time study was 6 years. There is little doubt that for those without experience of study since their last full-time course, insecurity about rusty 'study skills' is likely to be a significant problem. Most of the respondents had, however, engaged in some form of part-time study before joining their part-time degree course.

Table 2.18   Years since last
full-time study.

Years	%
Under 2	15
2–3	14
4–6	23
7–10	19
Over 10	30
Total	101

Table 2.19 Previous experience of part-time education.

Type of education	%[a]
Part-time day release	51
Evening classes	51
Correspondence courses	12
Extramural or WEA	4
Armed services courses	3
Block release	0[b]
Other	5
None	35

[a] Students were asked to indicate all that apply.
[b] Less than 0.5 per cent.

Previous experience of part-time study

A total of 65 per cent of the respondents had undertaken some form of part-time study before enrolling on their part-time degree course (Table 2.19). Part-time day release and evening classes were by far the most commonly encountered forms of previous part-time study. This suggests that the majority of the students enrolling on part-time degree courses have a reasonable idea of what they are letting themselves in for.

Of those who had previous experience of part-time study:

1. For the majority it was relatively recent. In fact, the average (median) gap between enrolling on their current course and being previously engaged in part-time study was one year.
2. It typically included at least one part-time course leading to some form of 'recognized qualification or certificate'. This was the case for 83 per cent of those with previous experience of part-time study. A substantial proportion of these (41 per cent) had undertaken two or more previous courses of part-time study leading to some form of certificate.

Of those who had previous experience of part-time study leading to a recognized qualification or certificate, most (77 per cent) had successfully *completed* the previous part-time courses. However, such courses would probably have been shorter and of a lower level of academic difficulty than their degree level studies.

Previous study at the same college

Over 30 per cent of the students had experience of previous study at the same college. Previous study at the same college seems to be a very significant route onto part-time degree courses. Those concerned with 'academic drift' would presumably infer from this that the maintenance of non-degree part-time courses is likely to be important to healthy enrolments on part-time courses at degree level.

Other concurrent courses

It is very unusual for students on part-time degree courses to be taking any other courses concurrently. This is not surprising in view of the simultaneous demands of degree level study, full-time employment and domestic responsibilities. Less than 5 per cent of the respondents (136 students) were taking any other concurrent course. Of these, 11 were completing full-time courses and the remainder were undertaking some form of part-time course. The survey did not explore the relationship between these 'concurrent' courses and the subjects of the students' part-time degree courses.

Educational qualifications at entry

The picture so far is of a population of part-time students in which the average school leaving age is low but with substantial post-school full-time education and extensive part-time education before enrolment on part-time degree level studies. Table 2.20 shows how this activity was converted into educational qualifications. The general impression given is that the respondents had already reached a relatively high educational level before embarking on their part-time degree courses. Table 2.20 also shows the wide diversity of the entry qualifications held by part-time undergraduates.

Table 2.20   Level of highest educational qualification attained (self and spouse).

Qualification	Self (%)	Spouse (%)
Postgraduate degree or postgraduate diploma	2	7
First degree	6	12
Professional qualifications at or above degree level	5	7
Open University credits	1	1
University or CNAA certificate or diploma	2	1
Teaching certificate or diploma	15	7
HNC/HND or BEC/TEC Higher National	34	5
Professional qualifications below degree level	5	6
GCE 'A' level[a] (two or more subjects) or Higher School Certificate	13	6
ONC/OND or BEC/TEC National	4	3
GCE 'A' level (one subject)	3	2
GCE 'O' levels (or CSE grade 1)	5	21
Other (including no formal qualifications)	5	22
Total	100	100

[a] Or Scottish Highers.

Table 2.21   GCE 'A' level scores.

'A' level point scores	Part-time CNAA undergraduates (%)	Full-time CNAA undergraduates (%)
Three 'A' levels		
13–15	9	3
9–12	30	18
3–8	62	79
Two 'A' levels		
8–10	6	5
5–7	51	39
2–4	43	56
Total		
%	101	100
No.	96 800	2696

Source: FESR (1981, 1982, 1983).

The most common entry qualifications were BTEC Higher awards (or equivalent), which were held by 34 per cent of the respondents. Results from the 1983 Further Educational Statistical Record (FESR) show, in fact, that the overwhelming majority of the students in this entry category (83 per cent) held HNCs rather than HNDs. This is confirmed in our survey by the fact that a similar proportion had completed part-time rather than full-time courses since leaving school. Some of the part-time degree courses are *designed* to follow on from HNC courses. A total of 15 per cent of the respondents held teaching qualifications and 13 per cent held 'A' levels. For none of the other categories does the percentage reach double figures.

The survey did not seek information on the GCE 'A' level grades of those that entered on the basis of 'A' levels, but relevant information is available from the FESR. As Table 2.20 shows, the proportion who enter part-time degree courses on the basis of GCE 'A' levels is not large (13 per cent of the respondents), and therefore the results from the FESR for 1981, 1982 and 1983 were combined to produce statistically reliable numbers. Part-time students were more likely than full-time students to have only two 'A' levels (40 and 52 per cent respectively), rather than three 'A' levels. However, within each of the two and three 'A' level categories, the part-time students had grades that were a little better than the full-time students (Table 2.21).

Unfortunately, it is not possible to identify the GCE 'A' levels obtained on the basis of part-time study from those obtained on the basis of full-time study. Presumably, however, the incidence of 'A' levels resulting from previous part-time study are higher for the part-time undergraduates.

Less than 1 per cent of the respondents held Open University credits. These students presumably received exemption from some part of their courses. It might be inferred from this low percentage that credit transfer is not yet as well-developed as it might be. However, the recent moves towards development

Table 2.22   The educational qualifications of part-time CNAA undergraduates compared with those of the adult population.

Level of qualification	CNAA part-time undergraduates (%)	Adult population[a] (%)
First or higher degree	13	3
Above 'A' level but below degree level	60	5
'A' level or equivalent	21	5
Below 'A' level	6	87

[a]Those aged 20 or over in England and Wales in 1971 (Qualified Manpower Survey).

of regional and national credit accumulation and transfer schemes are addressing this issue. It would be interesting to know what percentage of Open University students obtain credit on the basis of partial completion of a CNAA part-time degree course.

The proportions of spouses with postgraduate qualifications, first degrees and professional qualifications at or above degree level each exceed the corresponding proportions for the part-time undergraduates themselves. Is this evidence of some of the part-time students seeking to attain the same educational qualifications as of their spouses?

The proportion of part-time undergraduates holding entry qualifications below that of two GCE 'A' levels is only 13 per cent – and this includes the 'other' category. There is an indication here that non-standard entry ('students not holding the normal minimum entry qualifications for admission to a first degree or DipHE courses set out in Regulation 8.13 of CNAA's Principles and Regulations 1979 or equivalent qualifications': Evans, 1984) are less well-represented among part-time students than is sometimes believed. This is emphasized by comparing the results of our respondents with the Qualified Manpower Survey for 1971 (which corresponds to the year in which a large group of the students in our survey would have left school) (Table 2.22).

From one perspective, it appears that part-time degrees are playing a significant role in enabling those who are already well-educated to engage in continuing education. This presumably includes significant numbers who wish to update their knowledge and extend their range of educational attainment into areas that meet new and changed needs. From another perspective, it may suggest that admissions tutors are unduly conservative in their admissions policies. In particular, it may indicate a reluctance (or lack of the necessary expertise) to give credit for experiential learning.

Part-time and full-time students compared

The diversity of the entry qualifications held by the part-time undergraduates is particularly apparent when compared to the full-time students (Table 2.23). In terms of entry qualifications, GCE 'A' levels account for the overwhelming

Table 2.23 Entry qualifications: Part-time and full-time undergraduates.

	CNAA part-time undergraduates (%)	CNAA full-time undergraduates[a] (%)	University undergraduates[b] (%)
First or higher degree	8	3	0[c]
Cert. Ed./Dip. Ed.	15	0[c]	0[c]
HNC or HND	34	2	1
Two or more 'A' levels	13	74	91
ONC or OND	4	5	1
One 'A' level	3	6	1
Other	23	10	6
Total	100	100	100

[a] Entry qualifications of 1983 CNAA honours graduates of full-time and sandwich courses in England (*Source*: FESR).
[b] Entry qualifications of 1983 university undergraduates of UK universities (*Source*: USR).
[c] Less than 0.5 per cent.

majority of university entrants (over 90 per cent) and to a lesser extent CNAA full-time (and sandwich) degree course entrants. This may, of course, be a reflection of the average age of the entrants rather than the mode of study. In order to test this proposition, Table 2.24 compares the results of the survey with those of *mature* students enrolled on full-time CNAA degree courses.

Table 2.24 Level of highest educational qualification attained: Part-time and full-time mature students.

Qualification	Part-time (%)	Full-time[a] (%)
Postgraduate degree or postgraduate diploma	2	0
First degree	6	2
Professional qualifications at or above degree level	5	3
University or CNAA certificate or diploma[b]	3	3
Teaching certificate or diploma	15	4
HNC/HND or BEC/TEC Higher National	34	5
Professional qualifications below degree level	5	12
GCE 'A' level[c] (two or more subjects) or Higher School Certificate	13	38
ONC/OND or BEC/TEC National	4	6
GCE 'A' level (one subject)	3	10
GCE 'O' levels (or CSE grade 1)	5	13
Other (including no formal qualifications)	5	3
Total	100	99

[a] *Source*: Woodley (1987: based on returns from 171 students).
[b] Including Open University credits.
[c] Or Scottish Highers.

Table 2.25   Highest educational qualification: Open University and CNAA part-time undergraduates.

Qualification	CNAA part-time (%)	Open University[a] (%)
Postgraduate degree or postgraduate diploma	2	1
First degree	6	6
Professional qualifications at or above degree level	5	1
University or CNAA diploma (incl. OU credits)[b]	3	6
Teaching certificate or equivalent	15	18
HNC/HND or BEC/TEC Higher National	34	11
Professional qualifications below degree level	5	1
GCE 'A' level[c] (two or more subjects) or Higher School Certificate	13	12
ONC/OND or BEC/TEC National	4	8
GCE 'A' level (one subject)	3	7
GCE 'O' levels (or CSE grade 1)	5	20
Other (including no formal qualifications)	5	10
Total	100	101

[a] All registered students in 1984.
[b] For CNAA part-time results only.
[c] Or Scottish Highers.

Comparing Tables 2.23 and 2.24, it is clear that the pattern of entry qualifications of CNAA part-time students is closer to that of mature students than that of their school leaver colleagues. There are, however, still some notable differences. In general, the part-time students hold higher qualifications at entry than the mature full-time students. More specifically, they are much more likely to have been admitted on the basis of HNC or a teaching qualification rather than 'A' levels.

Open University and CNAA part-time undergraduates

It is probable that differences in the distributions of subjects account, in large part, for the differences in pattern of entry qualifications shown in Table 2.25. In particular, the impact of the large proportion of HNCs (a prerequisite for some of the CNAA courses) on the figures in the first column should be appreciated. Nevertheless, the figures do show that the proportion of students not holding the conventional 'minimum entry requirements' for a degree level course is much higher for the Open University students (37 per cent) than the CNAA part-time students (13 per cent).

The above analysis has been conducted at an aggregate level. When the respondents were disaggregated by subject area, significant differences emerged in the pattern of entry qualifications.

Variation across subject groups

The most dramatic differences across the subject groups arise where part-time courses are designed to follow other advanced courses of higher education. Thus the variation in the proportions of students with teaching qualifications range from 75 per cent in education to 1 per cent in engineering/technology. And the proportions of students with HNC/HND (or similar) range from 72 per cent in engineering/technology to one per cent in education.

It would appear that the proportions of part-time students with the very highest qualifications (postgraduate qualifications, professional qualifications at or above degree level and first degree) is highest in the less vocationally orientated subject areas. Thus the percentages with these qualifications in

Table 2.26 Level of highest qualification by subject group.

	Arts and humanities (%)	Social studies (%)	Education (%)	Science (%)	Engineering/ technology (%)	Business Studies (%)
Postgraduate degree or postgraduate diploma	4	6	2	1	1	2
First degree	10	9	3	10	3	2
Professional qualifications at or above degree level	6	12	4	4	0^b	6
Open University credits	2	1	1	1	1	0^b
University or CNAA certificate or diploma	3	3	6	1	0^b	1
Teaching certificate or diploma	29	6	75	4	1	5
HND/HNC or BEC/TEC Higher National	2	5	1	57	72	28
Professional qualifications below degree level	4	11	6	2	2	8
GCE 'A' level[a] (two or more subjects) or Higher School Certificate	9	21	1	11	13	19
ONC/OND or BEC/ TEC National	4	5	0^b	3	3	8
GCE 'A' level (one subject)	9	3	0^b	1	1	5
GCE 'O' levels or CSE grade 1	10	11	0^b	1	0^b	9
Other (including no formal qualifications)	9	8	1	3	4	7
Total	101	101	100	99	101	100

[a] Or Scottish Highers.
[b] Less than 0.5 per cent.

Table 2.27   Non-standard entry: Subject groups.

Subject	% of respondents with entry qualifications of one 'A' level or less
Arts and humanities	28
Social studies	22
Business studies	21
Sciences	5
Engineering/technology	5
Education	1

arts/humanities, social studies and science are 20, 27 and 15 respectively, whereas the percentages in education, engineering/technology and business studies are 9, 4 and 10 respectively.

There is substantial variation across subject groups in the proportions of part-time undergraduates with non-standard entry qualifications. Summing the results shown in the bottom three rows of Table 2.26 gives the proportions with entry qualifications of one GCE 'A' level or less (Table 2.27). Arts and humanities, and social studies both have higher than average proportions of students with particularly high qualifications and with relatively low entry qualifications. It would be interesting to discover whether this wide variation results in difficulties in teaching the students together.

Table 2.28   Subject distribution: Open University and CNAA part-time students.

	Open University[a] (%)	CNAA part-time degrees[b] (%)
Arts	23	9
Business/management studies (inc. law)	0[d]	20
Educational studies	6	25
Science (inc. maths)	32	14
Social sciences	18	7
Technology	19	21
Other[c]	3	4
Total	101	100

[a] Undergraduate student courses by faculty. All registered students in 1984.
[b] Student enrolments. *Source*: CNAA Annual Report for 1984.
[c] Includes health and paramedical studies, professional and vocational studies and interfaculty studies.
[d] Less than 0.5 per cent.

Comparisons with Open University students

This section makes some further comparisons between the students enrolled on part-time degree courses at polytechnics and colleges and those enrolled with the Open University. First, however, it is worth comparing the subject range of the courses taken by the students (Table 2.28).

CNAA part-time degree provision is more concentrated within the areas of business/management studies, education and technology. Open University student courses are more concentrated within the areas of science (including mathematics), arts and the social sciences. On balance, the range of courses that are being pursued by CNAA part-time degree students are more vocationally orientated than on Open University undergraduate programmes.

Compared to Open University students, the CNAA part-time degree respondents contained a higher proportion who were male and a higher proportion who were younger. Both of these factors seem to be related to the fact that the range of available CNAA part-time degree courses is more vocationally orientated (Tables 2.29 and 2.30).

Differences in the range of available subjects probably also contribute to the variation in the distributions of occupations of those enrolled on CNAA and Open University undergraduate programmes for part-time students (Table 2.31). If attention is restricted to those occupations where the percentage figures differ by at least 3 per cent, it can be seen that the Open University undergraduate population contains a higher proportion of housewives and those not working for various reasons (e.g. retired, independent means, unemployed and students). By contrast, the CNAA part-time degree population contains a higher proportion of administrators, managers and technical personnel. Apart from differences in the range of available subjects, the main reason for these dissimilarities is probably simply the fact that distance learning is the primary teaching mode for the Open University in contrast to face-to-face tuition on the CNAA part-time degree courses.

The final comparison in this section looks at the age at which the students left full-time education. On average, this was lower for the Open University undergraduates than for the CNAA questionnaire respondents (Table 2.32). Half of the Open University undergraduates left full-time education at the age

Table 2.29   Gender: Open University and CNAA part-time students.

Gender	Open University[a] (%)	CNAA part-time degrees[b] (%)
Male	55	65
Female	45	35

[a] All registered students in 1984.
[b] Survey respondents ($n = 2876$).

Table 2.30　Age: Open University and CNAA part-time students.

Age	Open University[a] (%)	CNAA part-time degrees[b] (%)
Under 30	14	47
30–34	23	19
35–39	24	16
40–49	24	14
50–59	10	3
60–69	4	1
70 and over	1	0
Total	100	100
Median	35	30

[a] All registered students in 1984.
[b] Survey respondents (*n* = 2876).

Table 2.31　Occupation: Open University and CNAA part-time students.

Occupation	Open University[a] (%)	CNAA part-time degrees[b] (%)
Housewives	17	5
Armed forces	3	0[c]
Administrators and managers	4	13
Teachers and lecturers	17	18
The professions and the arts	11	11
Qualified scientists and engineers	4	6
Technical personnel: inc. data processing, draughtsmen and technicians	13	22
Electrical, electronic, metal machines, engineering and allied trades	4	4
Farming, mining, construction and other manufacturing	2	1
Communications and transport (air, sea, road and rail)	2	0[c]
Clerical and office staff	11	9
Shopkeepers, sales and services, sport and recreation workers	5	3
Retired, independent means, not working (other than housewives), students	6	3
Other	2	5
Total	101	100

[a] All registered students in 1984 (occupation at commencement of studies).
[b] Survey respondents (*n* = 2876).
[c] Less than 0.5 per cent.

Table 2.32   Age at completion of full-time education:
Open University and CNAA part-time students.

Age	Open University[a] (%)	CNAA part-time degrees[b] (%)
16 or under	37	27
17	13	11
18	15	21
19	5	7
20	5	7
21 or over	25	26
Total	100	99

[a] All registered students in 1984.
[b] Survey respondents ($n = 2876$).

of 17 or younger compared with 38 per cent of the CNAA part-time degree respondents. The reason(s) for this difference are not obvious, but it is presumably associated with the generally higher entry qualifications of the latter reported in the previous section of this chapter.

Summary

1. *Personal details.* The average (median) age of the part-time students was 30. Almost two-thirds of them were male. The ethnic origins of the respondents were overwhelmingly UK/European. Most were married and in paid employment. Of those who were married, most had spouses in paid employment. Over 40 per cent of the respondents had children. Most of the respondents reported that both parents had left school at the age of 15. Compared with their parents, few of the respondents were engaged in manual occupations.

The findings of this study are consistent with a picture in which taking a part-time degree course is part of a process of upward social and economic mobility. There is also a suggestion in the findings that a significant proportion of the part-time students are members of families in which continuing education is perceived as a route to enhanced economic life chances. There is also a suggestion in the findings that the students were continuing a process of upward socio-economic mobility started by their parents.

2. *Employment profile.* Overall, a disproportionately large proportion of the respondents were employed in the public sector. Of those employed in the private sector, manufacturing industry was over-represented and the service sector was under-represented. Large organizations accounted for a disproportionately large percentage of the respondents.

Most of the respondents reported records of employment stability. Less than

10 per cent of the respondents had changed job (employer) more than once in the 5 years before starting their part-time degree course. Less than 10 per cent of the respondents had changed their employer since starting their courses. Over 30 per cent of the respondents reported that they were members of a professional body or institute.

3. *Educational background.* A majority of the respondents left school at the age of 17 or younger. Indeed, almost half left school at the age of 16 or younger. Many of those who had left school at an early age proceeded to some form of other full-time study. Nevertheless, a sizeable 38 per cent had completed their initial full-time education at the age of 17 or less.

Apart from those who proceeded *directly* to some other form of full-time study on leaving school, another sizeable group reported that they had subsequently undertaken some form of full-time study. Together, these two groups comprised 47 per cent of the respondents. However, 18 per cent had started but not finished such courses.

Almost two-thirds of the respondents had undertaken some form of part-time study before enrolling on their part-time degree course. For most of them this experience had been relatively recent. Part-time day-release and evening classes were by far the most common forms of previous part-time study. Previous study at the same college seems to be a significant route into part-time degree courses. Over 30 per cent of the students had experience of previous study at the same college.

Overall, the findings give a picture of a population of part-time students in which the average school leaving age is low but with a fairly high incidence of post-school full-time education (often not completed) and extensive part-time education.

4. *Entry qualifications.* The findings on the 'highest educational qualification previously attained' revealed great diversity in entry qualifications, but with the majority having already attained a relatively high educational level. In general, the part-time students hold higher qualifications at entry than mature full-time students. The most common entry qualifications were BTEC Higher awards (or equivalent). Less than 1 per cent held Open University credits.

From one perspective, it would appear that part-time degrees are playing a significant role in enabling those who are already well-educated to engage in further continuing education. From another perspective, it would seem that admissions tutors are unduly conservative in their admissions policies.

There is a substantial variation across subject groups in the proportions of part-time undergraduates with non-standard entry qualifications. 'Arts and humanities', 'social sciences' and 'business studies' all have above average proportions of students with non-standard entry qualifications. 'Arts and humanities' and 'social studies' also have higher than average proportions of students with particularly *high* entry qualifications.

5. *Comparisons with the Open University.* The proportion of students not holding the conventional 'minimum entry qualifications' for a degree level course is lower among the CNAA part-time undergraduates (13 per cent) than among Open University students (37 per cent). Compared to the Open University undergraduate courses, CNAA part-time provision is more concentrated in the areas of business/management studies, education and technology as opposed to science, arts and the social sciences. On balance, the range of courses being pursued by CNAA part-time undergraduates are more vocationally orientated than on Open University undergraduate programmes.

Compared to the Open University students, the CNAA part-time degree respondents contained a higher proportion who were male and a higher proportion who were younger. The Open University undergraduate population contains a higher proportion of housewives and those who, for various reasons, are not working. By contrast, the CNAA part-time degree population contains a higher proportion of administrators, managers and technical personnel.

3 | Institutional Perspectives

The course leaders' views

This chapter looks at part-time degrees from the perspective of the course leaders. A questionnaire was sent to the individual course leaders of the 66 courses whose students were being surveyed. Fifty-five questionnaires were returned, a response rate of 83 per cent (one was not completed because the course in question was not recruiting any further intakes owing to low enrolment).

The purpose of the survey – as set out at the top of the first page of the questionnaire – was:

> to identify the patterns of provision, and the range of special facilities available, for students on part-time degree courses approved by the CNAA.

It was recognized, in compiling the questionnaire, that only some elements of institutional provision, such as teaching methods, lie within the powers of the staff immediately responsible for the course. Other elements, such as library opening hours, are more under the influence of the institution. And yet other factors are more the result of policies of external agencies such as the DES. Other developments lie within the province of more than one of these groups and possibly even other agencies (for example, the existence of an access course).

Recognizing these complexities, it was decided to compile a questionnaire comprising questions which course leaders could either answer directly from their own experience, or could easily obtain corroboration of their own understanding, should it be necessary (for example, refectory opening hours). For these reasons, detailed questions on the level of resources made available (such as the resource allocation 'weighting' of the course) were omitted. The areas chosen for investigation were: recruitment and admission, curriculum and assessment, student facilities and student support.

The aim of the exercise was not to produce a statistical analysis of responses to pre-selected items. Instead, it was to allow course leaders an opportunity, under certain headings, to describe in their own terms the more immediate environment within which the course was offered in the institution. The questions were therefore not followed by pre-coded responses. Respondents were given space to answer in their own way. This enabled some to supply additional information even when the question appeared to invite a simple 'yes/no' response. For example, to the question 'Is it possible for a student to transfer to a corresponding full-time course at your college?', one course leader – while answering 'Yes' – pointed out that the course was offered jointly with two other (London) polytechnics. Additional information of this kind clearly assists in understanding part-time courses in their appropriate context.

In addition to responding to the 25 issues raised by the questions, course leaders were invited to enclose a copy of the student application form used by their course (if different from the Polytechnics Central Admissions Service (PCAS) standard form). They were also invited to add any remarks that they wished to make, especially on any successful practices or innovations that they had introduced in relation to the course. Almost half took up this opportunity.

Before turning to the detailed findings, it is worth reiterating that there are various kinds of part-time courses and client groups. A key distinction is between those courses which are building on a definite base of knowledge and skills and those which make fewer demands on entry. The former type of course is found in the sciences, engineering/technology and education, while the latter are located in the other subject areas. Associated with the different intakes are different study patterns and course duration. Typically, a part-time course in, say, engineering, building on an HNC base, would be studied over a 3-year period. A part-time degree course in the humanities, on the other hand, would typically be studied in the evenings, and over a 5- to 6-year period.

Other differences across the range of courses are also apparent. For example, for some courses catering for students on day release from their employer, the provision of a 'hardship' fund to aid those meeting difficulties in paying fees was a non-issue, as their fees were being met by their employing organizations.

These observations indicate that the experience of being a part-time student varies considerably. At the risk of caricaturing a complicated situation, it is possible to identify two polar kinds of student. At one end, there are students, probably in their early or mid-20s, receiving employer support to attend a course that relates directly to their employment. These students are usually male with relatively few family responsibilities. At the other end of the spectrum, are adults in their late 20s or 30s with family commitments seeking the opportunity of experiencing higher education. These students are more likely to be female and the course is likely to represent a sharp break from daily experience. They are likely to be self-financed and making a considerable personal commitment to study on the course.

This is, of course, an oversimplified description of the part-time student population, but the point here is that in making sense of an institution's practices, it is necessary to remember that there are different kinds of courses on offer and they are intended for very different kinds of client groups.

Recruitment and admission

Questions on recruitment and admission comprised one-third of the question-naire. This emphasis flowed from a recognition of the current national policy debates, where part-time provision is often seen as a potential source of future expansion within higher education. These sentiments are sometimes voiced by those who see a shift from full-time provision as a way of saving expenditure while maintaining opportunities for access. They are also voiced by those who look to an overall expansion of the system.

Specific questions on demand for part-time provision – actual or potential – were not included in the questionnaire as responses would have been mostly speculative. Instead, questions were asked about institutions' policies and practices in this area, as they affected individual courses. The general aim here was to ascertain ways in which the public sector of higher education was making the admission of potential students into the system as effective and painless as possible.

Access courses

Access courses have a particular role to play in relation to part-time courses, because many of those wanting to study part-time will be returning to study a long time after their last period of formal education. As yet, however, for only a small proportion (15 per cent) was there an 'access or preparatory' course connected with the chosen area of study. This figure is, however, somewhat misleading, as 12 of the 54 courses were designed for an HNC/BTEC intake, while others indicated that access courses were in the process of being designed with local colleges of further education. It appears that access courses with specific links to part-time courses are growing, though not remarkably quickly.

Associate student schemes

The number of colleges that are operating an associate student scheme, or other kinds of opportunities for students to sample courses without enrolling for a qualification was more extensive, amounting to half of the courses sampled. In about 50 per cent of those cases, it was possible for students who then wished to transfer to the course itself to be credited with their success as associate students. Perhaps this greater provision of associate student schemes, as compared with access courses, is not surprising, as the admission of associate students to existing courses can be accomplished fairly readily. Mounting an access course and securing an interface with an institution of higher education is less easily managed. In any event, the associate student path, on this evidence, appears to offer a more useful route into higher education than is commonly supposed.

Admission with advanced standing

Under CNAA regulations, it is possible to admit individuals to a point later than the beginning of a course on the basis of successfully completed formal studies (e.g. the route for 'associate students' who later become registered students on the course) and also on the basis of a person's maturity and experience, provided that the admitting institution has evidence that the applicant is likely to succeed. Very often, individuals can point to a number of achievements in their lives, where valuable knowledge and skills have been acquired. Course leaders were, therefore, invited to indicate whether, and in what ways, they attempted to assess applicants' uncertificated knowledge.

About half of the respondents claimed to offer the opportunity for admission with advanced standing. This is, of course, to say nothing of the extent to which such an entry route is used.

Among those who offer the possibility of admission with advanced standing, it is noticeable that traditional methods of assessment for admission were employed, requiring the applicants to sit an examination or submit an essay on a set topic. In addition, references would also be taken up. There was little sign of any other methods to identify applicants' experiential learning, acquired informally and perhaps less easily demonstrable in formal assignments. This is not surprising: such techniques are new to the UK, and their validity remains a matter of debate. It is for this reason that the CNAA recently commissioned a project designed to assist institutions in developing reliable methods of evaluating the experiential learning of applicants.

Admissions interviews

From the course leaders' replies, the interview appears to be the most important part of the selection process for most part-time degree courses, especially for those courses not building on a specific platform of entry qualifications. Presumably, it provides a means of assessing important aspects of an application, such as the motivation of the candidate, that would be difficult to assess in other ways. It is clear that course leaders place much confidence in the interview as a selection instrument. How far this confidence is justified is debatable and no evidence was adduced to support this level of confidence. About 20 per cent had a policy of interviewing *all* applicants irrespective of their qualifications. Whether this is an effective use of staff time, and provides staff with reliable information on which to base a decision, are perhaps matters for further investigation.

Apart from its value as a selection device, an admission interview can also be used to convey information to applicants and can serve a counselling function to explore the extent to which the course is the most appropriate one to meet the needs of the applicant. For some courses, the formal interview was supplemented by one or more prior interactions – sometimes with other applicants – where information about the course and the institution was made available.

Application forms

Nearly half of the responding course leaders indicated that the application form used for their part-time course was no different from that used for full-time courses outside the clearing houses systems (the Polytechnics' Standard Application Form). It would seem that many part-time applicants are being asked to complete a long application form that was designed for completion by younger applicants to full-time courses. It might be worthwhile reflecting on how daunting this is for an adult attempting to re-enter education after a period of some years. Apart from its length, many sections are clearly either inappropriate to prospective part-time students or given undue emphasis. For example, one page is left blank for a referee's report by 'the Head of your school, Principal of your college, or other referee'.

Size and appearance

For just over 50 per cent of the courses in question, an application form different from that used for full-time courses is sent to inquirers. Though most part-time course application forms are printed on A4 paper, they can vary in size from one to seven sides of A4. Perhaps the most striking difference in the forms, however, is their quality and visual attractiveness. Some had been simply typed, probably within a departmental office, onto A4 and photocopied. Their plain and unattractive appearance – sometimes exacerbated by poor-quality photocopies – contrasted with others that had been professionally designed and printed to a high standard.

Certain matters of policy are readily apparent. First, institutions vary over whether the production of the part-time application form is an institutional or departmental matter. Where it is seen as an institutional matter, a common form is 'normally' in use across the whole institution. The qualification 'normally' is necessary because even where there is a common form in an institution, some departments are still – on the evidence of this study – able to act independently, by producing and issuing their own form. At one polytechnic, for example, a specially designed form was used for a BEd in-service course, even though the polytechnic's common application form was in use for other courses. It is doubtful whether the specially designed form was more successful in every way in obtaining the necessary information. It did not, for example, ask the candidate to name their employing LEA.

Secondly, where a common form is used across an institution, there is clearly greater uniformity both in the information sought from the candidates and in the evidence on which admissions decisions are taken. This may, of course, be at the expense of some information that individual courses would like. To some extent, this difficulty can be overcome by the use of generalized wording ('employer/LEA') or the inclusion of optional questions that only some will answer (e.g. schoolteachers supplying a DES reference number).

On balance, there would appear to be merit in an institution producing its own 'core' application form for use across all its part-time degree courses. The production of a well-designed, attractive and simple-to-use form bearing the formal imprimatur of the polytechnic or college may itself be an incentive for the form's completion. Individual courses can then append a sheet asking for further specific information.

Information sought

The variation in the information sought for entry to part-time courses is in marked contrast to the common application form in use for full-time courses in polytechnics (through PCAS). The returned part-time forms requested information on an average of 26 items (ranging from 14 to 28 items). Altogether, 72 different items appeared on the forms. These figures exclude the standard application form which has some 51 items (several of which appear in one of the application forms returned by the part-time degree course leaders).

There appears to be little consensus among courses and institutions as to the information needed from part-time applicants. The only items in common were surname, first name (variously described) and signature. None of the other items were to be found in every application form – even name of employing organization, LEA, occupation, examinations passed, present and past experience, and referees.

For the items that were normally included, the information was often sought in quite different ways. For example, whereas most forms required applicants to list their examination passes, a minority asked for all examinations taken to be listed 'including failures'. It was largely these forms that also provided much blank space in asking candidates to set out their entire educational history, since the age of 11.

Some forms provided relatively little space for applicants to describe their employment or professional experience, despite the fact that they might be expected to have spent more time in employment since the age of 11 than in formal education. Most forms permitted applicants to set out further information or to give reasons to support their application, but the space allowed was generally limited and applicants were seldom invited to attach additional sheet(s) if necessary. The kinds of information suggested for inclusion in these sections were also limited: candidates were not normally encouraged to identify their accomplishments (whether in work or elsewhere) or outline their aspirations for themselves.

Some institutions have found ways to obtain much useful information on just two sides of A4 with a form laid out clearly and undauntingly. However, many of the application forms were unattractive or failed to ask pertinent questions or asked for information in ways insensitive to prospective adult students. The key criterion for any application form is: Is it likely to encourage applicants to present themselves as well as possible and provide a basis on which to make an informed decision about the applicant concerned?

Enrolment and induction

Newly enrolled students receive a wide variety of forms of induction into the course and institution. In one case, no induction programme of any kind was provided, but this was for entry to a degree course building on a BTEC course provided by the same institution, which gave the staff an opportunity to talk informally to most of the intending students. At the other end of the spectrum, another institution offered a first-year 'half-credit' study skills course that included a section to ensure that students were able to make full use of the college's facilities and could manage and present their project work effectively.

Course guides

In between these extremes, a number of different strategies were adopted for imparting information to students about the course and the institution. The most common was the provision of a course guide, leaflet or brochure. This was provided by just over half of the 54 courses, though the format varied widely. Course leaders were not asked to send examples of their course guides, but some did. They ranged from a 6-page A5 leaflet to a 50-page A4 booklet, which not only described the elements of the course in considerable detail but also contained much information about the place of the course within the structure of the institution, a 'who's who' of staff associated with the course, and a set of notes on study skills.

Clearly, the production of such guides is resource-intensive, because much of the material is specific to the department and course concerned. Interestingly, therefore, no examples were provided of such course guides being an amalgam of course-specific information (provided by the department) and more general information provided centrally by the institution. The development of a 'core' document by the institution to which individual courses can append departmental and course-specific information might be considered as a means of providing a more effective service to the part-time students while offering resource savings to the institution.

Timing

Institutions vary as to the timing of giving information to new students. The interview was often seen as important here (22 per cent), despite the fact that students were then interacting with the institution in a different role (as applicant), the information was often imparted orally and it was some time before admission. It might be helpful here to distinguish between information that the applicants would need to assist them in deciding whether to accept an offer of a place on the course and that which can be more accurately described as induction information. Others saw the need to develop the new student's understanding of the course and the institution as a continuing process. Most took some responsibility for improving students' abilities to use the available resources effectively, whether institutional (such as the library) or departmental. Here again, there was wide variation: some provided brief induction programmes over a single day or evening (24 per cent), whereas others (26 per cent) put on a range of events over a week or at least more than one day.

Within the other 50 per cent of the courses, other strategies – apart from course guides and specific induction programmes – for imparting information and inducting students included presentations on study skills, a meeting with former students and providing students with past examination papers. For a very few, 'induction' was perceived as a continuing process and residential weekends and summer schools were seen as helpful.

Relationship with induction of full-time students

A separate issue is the extent to which such induction arrangements should be integrated with those provided for full-time students. There are differences of view here. Some course leaders believe that, as far as practicable, part-time students should feel themselves to be of equal status to full-time students and that the induction arrangements should be largely the same for all students. In practice, this may mean part-time students being expected to attend day-time events provided essentially for full-time students. No examples were given of full-time students being asked to attend evening induction sessions. On the other hand, some feel that part-time students require particular provision. Clearly, decisions here are partly affected by the actual timetable for the part-time course in question: students attending on an evening-only basis may need different kinds of arrangements from those attending on a day-release basis who may be integrated into the institution's general arrangements more easily.

Curriculum and assessment

The difference of view over whether or not part-time students should be afforded special kinds of provision or should be integrated into the mainstream of the institution's provision came through also in responses to questions concerning teaching and assessment patterns. In three of the courses, the formal sessions were fully integrated across the part-time and full-time modes.

Teaching methods

So far as teaching methods are concerned, the strategies were of two kinds. There were those which sought to give additional support to the part-time students through providing more handouts, or duplicated course notes, than for the full-time students. Only one-quarter of courses followed this path, as a matter of policy. Certainly, the added maturity and experience of part-time students were recognized to some extent, as ways were found (and this was the other strategy adopted) to draw on that experience within the course. A small but significant minority attempted deliberately to ensure that the course built on the students' work experience, including setting mini-projects to complete in the work situation. Another common method lay in the use of student-led seminars. Less common were the use of videos, extended essays, case studies, specially written coursework and learning packs, computer-assisted learning, independent study and distance learning.

This list of teaching and learning methods and styles should not mislead. Most course leaders referred to only one or two such strategies and over 25 per cent were unable to point to any special teaching methods adopted to meet the needs of part-time students. The general picture is of the occasional institution being particularly adventurous, experimenting with a variety of methods allowing part-time students to be active in their own learning arrangements and accomplishments, a majority of institutions who feel the need to pay attention to the particular requirements of part-time students in terms of teaching methods but with a limited repertoire of methods, and a significant minority who are not convinced that part-time students have needs that require a wider range of teaching/learning methods than those provided for full-time students.

Assessment

Patterns of assessment showed even less recognition of students' part-time mode of study. Among the particular methods employed, in descending order of use, were relatively greater use of continuous assessment, importance of project, open-book or previously-seen examinations, work-based assessments, case studies, negotiated assessments and (for one course) self-assessment. Where continuous assessment was used, its contribution to the total assessment ranged up to 100 per cent (for one course). Perhaps surprisingly, less than one-quarter of respondents cited its use, while one – again reflecting the feeling that part-time students should be treated like all other students – was adamant that continuous assessment was not to be used at all for the course in question.

A small number pointed to certain features of the assessment arrangements which recognized the additional constraints faced by many part-time students. Flexible deadlines for handing in assessed essays, and the ability to stretch the duration of taught units so that in turn the dates of formal assessments could be altered, were two such strategies.

Relationship with full-time courses

For some years there has been discussion about the resources made available to part-time courses. It is often suggested that the formulae by which resources are allocated to the polytechnics and colleges sector of higher education do not fairly reflect the actual level of resources required to offer part-time degree courses.

According to this argument, such courses can only be offered by utilizing the resource base provided for full-time courses. As a result, there has developed unwittingly – so it might seem – a move towards the situation envisaged in the Robbins Report (1963), which considered that part-time courses should be made available only where there was an existing successful full-time course.

The actual picture appears, however, to be rather different. Of the courses covered in the survey, opportunities for transfer to a corresponding full-time course were limited to just over half. And for only one-third of the courses, did the course leader consider that the full-time course was essential for the continued existence of the part-time course. In other words, there are prima facie indications that many part-time courses exist and are surviving on their own account, without being dependent on a parallel full-time course. How far this picture accurately reflects the situation nationally, and the extent to which it reflects deliberate policies of resource allocation within institutions, would need further study.

Student facilities

Advice and counselling

In terms of informal advisory arrangements, the results of the course leaders' questionnaire suggest that part-time students are well-served. All except two courses offered advisory or counselling services for students on the course, often in addition to the institution's own student counselling services. Nearly half of the respondents pointed to the central counselling services, over a half cited the use of personal tutors for students on the course, and in over a third the course leader or course tutor saw it as part of their role to provide a counselling service (sometimes with the support of a particular member of staff). For some courses, year tutors also serve in a counselling capacity. Many courses offer a range of these advisory services.

Again, though, the formal description covers a range not only of practices, but also of attitudes to supporting part-time students. For example, 'personal tutors' might have responsibility for a small group of students, or might have responsibility for a whole year. The actual availability of such staff for counselling purposes ranged from being 'always available' (which might in practice mean, for part-time students, rarely available), available just prior to the scheduled evening sessions, holding occasional meetings with groups of students and holding a termly meeting with each student. No mention was made of any of the staff with counselling responsibilities having had any training or staff development for that role. In other words, both the students' access to confidential advice and the quality of that advice are uncertain and might benefit from review by institutions.

Library facilities

A number of questions were asked in the questionnaire about the physical resources available to students on courses. For all but two of the courses, the library was open until at least 8.30 pm for 4 days of the week. A third enjoyed library facilities on the weekend with the library opening on Saturday mornings and for a very small group it was also open on Sundays.

An area of library provision where part-time students are possibly adversely affected is that of vacation opening. It was not clear whether the opening hours mentioned operated throughout the vacations, although it was stated occasionally that they did not. Institutions that do not open during vacations are perhaps forgetting that many part-time students remain in the locality during vacations and that access to an academic library is one means of sustaining part-time students' academic interests during the break in formal classes.

Some institutions recognize, in their library policy, that part-time students are not always able to gain access to the library and to turn round books as quickly as their full-time counterparts. A fifth of the courses reported an extended 'short loan' service for part-time students. Other services mentioned as being provided specially for part-time students were appropriate staff being on duty for part-time (evening) courses, extended borrowing periods, provision of special bookstock for use by part-time students, a postal service and telephone reservations.

Canteen refectory facilities

The canteen facilities, too, show signs of reflecting the needs of part-time students, though here there was more unevenness. Over 75 per cent of institutions' canteens were open until 6.30 pm, and 25 per cent were open after 6.30 pm. In nearly a quarter of institutions, however, students either had only machines to meet their needs for food and drinks, or – in three cases – had no facilities of any kind.

Communal areas

An absence of canteen facilities might be mitigated, if instead there was some form of common room or communal area, where students could mix if only briefly. Course leaders were asked to give an indication of any communal facilities available to students 'on this course (e.g. common rooms or other areas for informal activity *for part-time students*)'. Ten respondents pointed to some kind of communal area specially available to the course students. This included a foyer in the department, a 'large, modern and attractive coffee bar/lounge' and the 'use of the senior common room with comfortable armchairs and pleasant surroundings (officially not allowed)'. One course had enjoyed the use of a common room for part-time students, but it had been withdrawn after only a year's operation.

Nearly 75 per cent either responded that there were no special facilities available or that the students were able to use the general communal facilities available to the full-time students (including the student union facilities, to which nearly 25 per cent of the course leaders pointed).

Impact of resource constraints

A total of 60 per cent of the course leaders identified some kind of impact of reduced resources on the facilities for the students on their course. Care needs to be taken in interpreting the silence of the other 40 per cent, as the extent to which part-time courses have been 'protected' by intra-institutional resource allocation policies – through cross-subsidies for example – was not explored in the questionnaire.

The impact of resource problems was experienced in four areas. Impact on *staff resources* was seen in altered class contact time, reduced team teaching and a loss of visiting lecturers. *Limits on student intake numbers* affected the range of options, the modes of study (on one course a day-release mode had to be discontinued) and the pattern of course availability (for example, one course reported switching to an intermittent admissions cycle with a new cohort being recruited only every other year). Reduced *support services* were cited – the library, canteen and computer facilities were all mentioned. Finally, course leaders identified *physical resources* in terms of capital funds, teaching accommodation and social facilities.

Nevertheless, when asked to identify the impact of resource constraints, 40 per cent of the respondents remained silent. Perhaps the situation might reasonably be summarized by the observation that, although there has been some 'squeeze' for most courses, for others there has not been a major impact on provision. However, institutions have presumably been constrained in the extent to which they have been able to respond to any unmet demand for part-time higher education by expanding their provision of part-time degree courses.

Student involvement

In all but two courses, some more or less formal means was provided by which students could participate in the control and monitoring of the course. The normal mode lay in representation on the course committee, although other bodies such as the departmental board of studies or subject committees were also used. Of more interest here is the actual involvement in course decision making that this representation provides. Course committee involvement ranged from one or more student representatives drawn from each student cohort through to one student for the whole course. The frequency of meetings ranged between one and three meetings per year. In other words, 'student representation' could mean negligible participation in course control or it could mean substantial input from the students taking the course.

In addition to such participation in the formal structure of course management, on many courses staff use additional means of eliciting feedback from students. A student questionnaire is used in about 10 per cent of courses and other means include various kinds of student meetings where staff may or may not be present (these meetings go under such names as the student forum or liaison committee or were simply annual meetings of the whole class). How far these various methods resulted in an input of student views into the formal evaluation process is unclear. The involvement of the students in course evaluation was explicitly mentioned by only a tiny minority, and it may be that whatever the quality of staff–student interaction, course teams might wish to reflect on ways in which student feedback can be more systematically incorporated into the course evaluation process. However, as one course leader suggested, this might be a 'problem area' for part-time students who prefer informal discussion rather than involvement in formal procedures, which are often time-consuming and most commonly held during the day.

Social identity

So far as the students' social identity is concerned, there was a sharp difference in views among the course leaders. They differ about 50:50 over whether they feel responsibilities towards promoting social interaction with and among the students. Many put on occasional social events, often financing them out of their own pockets. Strongly evident in these activities was a divide between subject areas. Those who offer no such happenings were almost all in the sciences and engineering/technology. Most, though not all, of those who took social interaction seriously were to be found in the social sciences and the humanities. As many of the respondents pointed out, social interaction could be developed through the course itself in group work, on residential weekends, via summer schools and on field trips (where courses in some of the sciences are especially well-placed).

Study skills

The subject divide (broadly science and non-science) also emerged in relation to study skills. Again, there were equal numbers of courses where either there was a study skills course or advice was available on request (often the student is referred to the institution's counselling services), or no such assistance appears to be available. Of those falling into this last category, all but two were in the areas of the sciences or engineering/technology. It should be recalled that many of the part-time degree courses in these areas recruit from those holding BTEC certificates and so are building on a more or less common platform. The need for study skills, in these circumstances, is obviously reduced (though not removed).

The development of study skills took many forms. In length, they ranged from a single day-long session to a full two-term programme. In format, particularly where available on request, they included self-learning packs, booklets and other handouts. Occasionally, this provision was under the direction of the library or the institution's educational development service. Whoever is responsible for its provision, and whatever its format, it should presumably be appropriate to the likely level of need. Even allowing for the different recruitment patterns of part-time courses, it appears that provision in this area could benefit from review. Central services are unlikely to provide sufficient service by themselves: the study skills required of students vary across subjects and in relation to course objectives.

Non-completion

A key issue concerning part-time courses concerns the cost to the system. An important factor in those costs and in the general effectiveness of part-time degree courses is their 'non-completion rates' (the proportion of students who do not, for whatever reason, complete the course on which they were first registered). Only 20 per cent of the course leaders were unable to point to any special procedures designed to lessen non-completion. Most course leaders were very aware of non-completion as an issue and one to which effort needs to be addressed.

Four kinds of strategy were identified. First, *flexibility* could be built into the course structure. For example, a modular structure could allow students to choose the order in which modules were taken or it might be possible, as part of the design of the course, to allow students to intercalate a period away from the course. Secondly, *assessment regulations* could also allow flexibility while maintaining standards. For example, flexible timetables for handing in assessed assignments or provision to carry forward 'failed' credits were among those mentioned. Thirdly, providing students with *information* about the course is taken to be very important by some course leaders. Finally, and perhaps most significantly, on some courses *staff* exercise a collective personal responsibility towards the students, being readily available for consultation and also monitoring students' attendance carefully and following up non-attendance (with employers if necessary) assiduously.

Difficulty in meeting course *fees* is, of course, one possible reason for non-completion – particularly on those courses where the proportion of self-financing students is relatively high. For well over half of the courses, some kind of 'hardship' fund was available, while among the remainder students were often sponsored by employers. Surprisingly, only two course leaders indicated the presence of a 'payment by instalment' scheme. Another means of lightening the financial burden lies, as one course leader observed, through tax relief being given for fees paid by part-time students.

Summary

This chapter presents the findings of a questionnaire distributed to the course leaders of the 66 courses whose students were being surveyed. The purpose of this questionnaire was to identify the patterns of provision, and the range of special facilities available, for part-time undergraduates. The response rate was over 80 per cent.

In interpreting the findings, it is necessary to bear in mind that there are different kinds of courses on offer and that they are intended for very different kinds of client groups.

1. *Access.* Access courses with specific links to part-time degree courses are growing, though not remarkably quickly. As yet, only about 15 per cent of the courses have an 'access or preparatory' course associated with the under-graduate programme.

About half of the courses sampled pointed to an associate student scheme or other kinds of opportunities for students to sample courses without enrolling for a qualification. In about half of those cases, it was possible for students who then wished to transfer to the course itself to be credited with their success as associate students. The associate student path, on this evidence, appears to offer a more useful route into part-time higher education than is often appreciated.

2. *Admission with advanced standing.* About half of the respondents claimed to offer the opportunity for admission with advanced standing. However, CNAA figures suggest that the actual number admitted with advanced standing is very small. For those who offer the possibility of admission with advanced standing, traditional methods of assessment for admission were normally employed.

3. *Interviews.* Very heavy reliance is placed on the interview in the selection process, especially for those courses not building on a specific platform of entry qualifications. About 20 per cent of the respondents had a policy of interviewing *all* applicants irrespective of their entry qualifications.

4. *Application Forms.* Nearly half of the responding course leaders indicated that the application form used was no different from that used for full-time courses. It would seem that many part-time applicants are being asked to complete a long application form that was designed for completion by younger applicants to full-time courses.

Where specially designed application forms are used for part-time courses, there is wide variation in their size and visual attractiveness. There is also wide variation in the information sought. On the application forms that were available from the course leaders, the number of separate items ranged from 14 to 28 and covered 72 *different* items, indicating little consensus as to the information needed from part-time applicants.

5. *Induction.* There is great variety in the provision of induction to the course and institution ranging from one course (building on a BTEC course provided at the same institution) with no induction programme, to one course that integrated induction into a first-year 'half credit' study skills course. Some courses provided brief induction programmes over a single day (24 per cent), whereas others (26 per cent) put on a range of events lasting from more than one day to up to a week.

6. *Information for students.* The most common form of providing information to new students was some form of course guide. Course guides ranged from a 6-page A5 leaflet to a 50-page A4 booklet giving in great detail the elements of the course, the place of the course within the structure of the institution, a 'who's who' of the staff associated with the course, and a set of notes on study skills.

Other strategies for providing information to new students – apart from course guides and specific induction programmes – included presentations on study skills, a meeting with former students and providing students with past examination papers. For a very few courses, 'induction' was perceived as a continuing process and residential weekends and summer schools were seen as helpful.

7. *Special provision for part-time students.* Some course teams appear to believe that part-time undergraduates should, as far as practicable, be integrated with full-time students, and this view was manifest in common induction programmes and common formal classes. On the other hand, some course teams feel that the needs of part-time students are very different and they require particular provision.

8. *Teaching/learning methods.* So far as special teaching methods for the part-time students were concerned, there were two main strategies. First, particular support was given through the provision of more handouts or duplicated notes than those provided to full-time students. Secondly, ways were found of drawing on the experience of the part-time students within the course. This included setting mini-projects to complete in the work situation, student-led seminars and, less commonly, greater use of videos, extended essays, case studies, specially written coursework and learning packs, computer-assisted learning, independent study and distance learning.

The general picture is of the occasional courses being particularly adventurous, experimenting with a wide variety of teaching methods to enable part-time students to take a more active role in their own learning, a majority of courses who feel the need to pay attention to the particular needs of part-time students but with a limited awareness or repertoire of teaching/learning methods, and a significant minority who are not convinced that part-time students have needs that require a different range of teaching/learning methods than those provided for full-time students.

9. *Assessment.* Patterns of assessment showed even less recognition of the students' part-time mode of study. Among the particular methods employed, in descending order of use, were relatively greater use of continuous assessment, importance of project, open-book or previously seen examinations, work-based assessments, case studies, negotiated assessments and (for one course) self-assessment. In addition, flexible deadlines for handing in assessed work and the ability to stretch the duration of taught courses (so that in turn the dates of formal assessments could be altered) were also reported.

10. *Transfer opportunities.* Opportunities to transfer to a corresponding full-time course was limited to just over 50 per cent of the courses. For only one-third of the courses did the course leader consider that the full-time course was essential to the continued existence of the part-time course.

11. *Counselling.* Almost half of the course leaders pointed to the institution's central counselling services as available to the part-time students. All but two of the courses offered advice and counselling services to students by staff on the course, in addition to any provided by the institution's central counselling service. No mention, however, was made of any of the course staff having any training or staff development for undertaking such a role.

12. *Library provision.* For all but two of the courses, the library was open until at least 8.30 pm for 4 days of the week. A third of the courses enjoyed some library facilities on the weekend. Some institutions show an appreciation, in their library regulations, that part-time students are not always able to gain access to the library and turn round books as quickly as their full-time counterparts. A fifth of the courses reported an extended 'short loan' service for part-time students. Other services mentioned as being provided specially for part-time students were appropriate staff being on duty for evening courses, extended borrowing periods, provision of special bookstock for use by part-time students, a postal service and telephone reservations.

13. *Refectory.* Over 75 per cent of the institutions had refectories open until 6.30 pm, and 25 per cent were open after 6.30 pm. In nearly 25 per cent of the institutions, however, students either had only machines to meet their needs for food or drinks, or – in the case of three courses – had no facilities of any kind.

14. *Resource constraints.* A total of 60 per cent of the course leaders identified at least some impact of resource constraints in recent years on the facilities for the students on their courses. Four main areas were mentioned: staff resources (e.g. reduced team teaching and loss of visiting lecturers), limits on student intake numbers, reduced support services and physical resources.

15. *Course review.* In all but two courses, some formal means was provided by which students could participate in the control and monitoring of their course. This usually meant representation on the course board or committee. The

involvement of the students in course evaluation, however, was explicitly mentioned by only a small minority of the course leaders.

16. *Student cohesion.* Course leaders seem to split about 50:50 over whether they feel responsibilities for promoting social interaction with and among the students. Strongly evident in this split was a divide between subject areas. Those who do not seek to promote such social interaction were almost all found in the sciences and engineering/technology. In the social sciences and humanities, course leaders mentioned various ways of developing social identity among the students within the course itself in group work, on residential weekends, via summer schools and on field trips.

17. *Study skills.* The subject divide (broadly science and non-science) also emerged in relation to study skills. Provision for the development of study skills was mostly found outside of the sciences and engineering/technology. Sometimes, the study skills provision was under the direction of the library or the institution's educational development unit. It took many forms, from programmes of various duration (one day to a full two-term course unit) to self-learning packs and other forms of handouts.

18. *Non-completion.* Most of the course leaders were very aware of non-completion as an issue to which effort needed to be directed. Only 20 per cent were unable to point to any special procedures or practices designed to lessen non-completion. These largely fell into four categories: flexibility in terms of course structure, flexibility in terms of assessment procedures, measures to ensure that new students are well-informed about the course, and the exercise by staff of a collective responsibility for monitoring student attendance and progress.

19. *Financial support.* For over half of the courses there exists some kind of 'hardship' fund for students who encounter difficulty with their fees. Only two course leaders indicated the presence of a 'payment-by-instalment' scheme.

4 | The Decision to Enrol

Aims in enrolling

The students' questionnaire contained a list of possible aims and the students were invited to indicate how important each was in their decision to enrol (Table 4.1). The improvement of career prospects was selected as the main aim by more than three times the number of respondents that selected any other one of the aims listed. Although Table 4.1 shows the aims that were regarded as most important, it obscures information on other aims that the students viewed as important. For this reason, the questionnaire also asked respondents to indicate the importance of each factor separately. The aims were grouped into

Table 4.1   Main aim when enrolling.

Aims	%
Improve career prospects	39
Demonstrate ability to complete course	12
Promotion/increased salary in present work	9
Learn more about subject	9
Increase job changing opportunities	8
Develop mind	5
Improve present job performance	4
Widen horizons	4
Compensate for lack of previous educational opportunities	3
Qualification for higher level course	3
Acquire self-confidence	1
Relief from usual surroundings/responsibilities	1
Benefit children's education	0[a]
Make new friends with similar interests	0[a]
Shared interest with spouse/friend	0[a]
Other	2
Total	100

[a] Less than 0.5 per cent of respondents.

work-related aims, subject-related aims, personal development aims and more general aims. Some aims were clearly inapplicable to some of the students (e.g. 'to benefit my children's education' was only applicable to students with children!), so that those who selected the 'not applicable' response were excluded before the percentages were computed (Table 4.2).

Each of the work related aims was clearly important to a large proportion of the students. The improvement of career prospects (either in the student's current employment or as a basis for employment mobility) was of primary importance. Only 6 per cent of the students rated 'To improve my career prospects' as 'not important'. The least important work-related aim was 'To help me do my present job better' – this was rated as 'very important' by less

Table 4.2 Importance attached to aims on enrolling.

Aims	Very important (%)	Fairly important (%)	Not important (%)
Work-related aims			
To improve my career prospects	76	19	6
To improve my chance of promotion/ increased salary in my present type of work	61	24	16
To increase the opportunities for changing my job	60	27	13
To help me do my present job better	38	37	25
Subject-related aims			
To learn more about a subject that interests me	55	39	7
To get an educational qualification for a higher level course	41	26	33
To develop a shared interest with my spouse partner, friend, etc.	4	17	79
Personal development aims			
To prove to myself (or others) that I could complete a degree course	50	29	22
To widen my horizons	46	41	13
To develop my mind	42	43	14
To acquire more self-confidence	23	36	41
General aims			
To make up for lack of educational opportunities in the past	32	28	40
To benefit my children's education	13	32	55
To get away from my usual surroundings and responsibilities at home	9	19	73
To make new friends with similar interests	6	28	66

Note: Horizontal percentages sum to 100 per cent.

than 40 per cent of the students. It would seem that part-time degree courses, even in non-vocationally orientated subjects, are valued as qualifications for enhancing economic life chances.

Interest in acquiring a qualification for career advancement is different, of course, from subject interest *per se*. For 7 per cent of the respondents, interest in the subject was rated as not important, 39 per cent reported that it was fairly important and the remaining 55 per cent reported that it was very important. The other subject-related aim that was rated as 'very important' by a substantial proportion of the respondents (41 per cent) was 'To get an educational qualification for a higher level course'. This finding has important implications for the availability of higher degrees by part-time study and will be discussed in more detail later when findings concerning students' future educational plans are addressed.

A substantial proportion of the respondents rated all of the personal development aims as important. Of this group of aims, the most important was to demonstrate the ability to complete a degree course. This was rated as 'very important' by half of the students and it was the second most frequently cited 'main aim'. Of the remaining aims (those contained in the 'general' category), only 'compensation for lack of previous educational opportunities' was reported to be 'very important' by a substantial proportion of the respondents.

Future educational plans

It was reported in the previous section that a 'very important' reason for obtaining a part-time degree for over 40 per cent of the respondents was to get an educational qualification for a higher level course. A further 26 per cent rated this as simply 'important'. In view of this, it is appropriate to deal with the respondents' future educational plans at this point. The questionnaire asked the respondents to indicate any further study/training that they envisaged after completing their part-time degree course. The respondents could indicate more than one type of further study/training, so that the percentages shown in Table 4.3 total to more than 100 per cent.

Table 4.3   Further study/training envisaged after present course.

Qualification	%
Examinations of a professional body or institute	40
Taught master's degree	35
Postgraduate research degree (e.g. MPhil or PhD)	23
Professional updating course	20
Postgraduate diploma	16
Teacher training	12
Another first degree	9
Other	6

Table 4.4 Interest in more advanced part-time study at same college.

Qualification	%[a]
Postgraduate diploma (on the basis of 1–2 years of part-time study)	24
Taught master's degree (on the basis of 2–3 years of part-time study)	37
Postgraduate research degree (e.g. MPhil or PhD)	26
None of the above	41

[a] The column total exceeds 100 per cent as the respondents were able to indicate all the categories that applied to them.

A total of 40 per cent of the respondents envisaged undertaking further study for the examinations of a professional body. This, in fact, understates the extent to which the respondents expected to use their degree qualification to join, obtain exemption from, or gain higher status in a professional body relevant to their career, because some professional bodies do not require further examinations. When this question was posed directly in the questionnaire, 48 per cent said that they would seek to use their degree qualification in this way (24 per cent said that they did not intend to do so, leaving 28 per cent answering 'don't know').

The number of respondents who envisaged higher level academic study was also high: 35 per cent in the case of taught masters' degrees and 23 per cent in the case of research degrees. Moreover, this presumably excludes those who would wish to do so but who were not aware of available courses that would meet the practical requirements of part-time students within a feasible distance. This possibility was anticipated when the questionnaire was designed, and so the next question asked 'Would you be interested in proceeding to further part-time study for a postgraduate Diploma, taught Master's degree or postgraduate research degree (e.g. MPhil or PhD) in your present (or closely related field of study) if this were possible at the college at which you are currently enrolled?' Not surprisingly, the positive responses increased (Table 4.4).

The majority of the respondents expressed some positive interest in proceeding to further part-time study for a higher level academic award *if this were possible at the college at which they were currently enrolled*. This will be good news to those engaged in the development of postgraduate part-time courses for whom information on potential demand is notoriously difficult to obtain. It also emphasizes the value of the coexistence of part-time courses at different levels within the same institution.

Sources of information

The sources from which the respondents first heard about their courses are shown in Table 4.5. Presumably, most of the 22 per cent of the students who first

Table 4.5   How students first heard about their course.

Source of information	%
College prospectus	22
Local press	19
Colleague(s) at work	19
Employer	13
From staff of the college running the course	12
Someone currently (or previously) enrolled on the course	11
Relative or friend outside of work	6
Poster about the course	4
Local library	3
Specialized careers advice service for adults	1
Club/organization to which you belong	0[a]
Radio/television	0[a]
Total	110[b]

[a] less than 0.5 per cent.
[b] Some respondents indicated more than one source.

heard about their courses via college prospectuses would have been through student-initiated enquiries.

Of the formal information channels (local press, posters, local library, specialized career service for adults and radio/television), only the local press accounts for a substantial percentage (19 per cent) of the responses. Informal channels (colleagues at work, friends, relatives and someone currently or previously enrolled on the course) account for 36 per cent of responses. Finally, employers and contacts with staff actually running the course account for a further 25 per cent of the responses.

It is important to appreciate that Table 4.5 does not show what are the best ways of disseminating information about part-time degree courses, but simply how part-time degree students currently hear about their courses. Thus, for example, the low figure for 'specialized careers advice service for adults' presumably reflects the lack of availability of such services or lack of awareness of them. Percy *et al.* (1982) have shown that the provision in this area is thin and uneven. There is little doubt that awareness of the opportunities for part-time degree study outside of the Open University is very limited indeed. Moreover, an HMI Report on part-time advanced courses in the public sector of higher education (DES, 1985) asserted that more students could be accommodated at a low *marginal* cost. While it is clear that the market for part-time courses is local, the scale of part-time degree provision nationally has now reached a level where there would appear to be a prima facie case for some central initiative in disseminating information. This would not, of course, eliminate the need for local efforts at the course level but it would probably have a significant positive impact on the effectiveness of those efforts.

Barriers to enrolment

About 75 per cent of the students were unaware of the existence of their course for more than 2 years before they enrolled. This would appear to be further evidence of a lack of general awareness of the availability of part-time degree courses within polytechnics and other colleges of higher education. Of the remaining 25 per cent, the three main reasons given for not enrolling earlier were:

1. Lacked the necessary educational background/qualifications (38 per cent).
2. Prevented by work commitments (18 per cent).
3. Prevented by family commitments (9 per cent).

Less than 1 per cent cited 'financial reasons'.

Most staff involved in the provision of part-time degree courses have views on the barriers to access to such courses. The views that are most important, however, are those of potential students not enrolled. This survey took a step towards the latter by seeking the views of students *currently* enrolled. The results are shown in Table 4.6.

It should be appreciated in interpreting these results that they are not statements of fact but students' perceptions. Moreover, they are the views of those who gained access rather than those who did not. Of those students who expressed a view on each of the above factors, most saw the lack of course availability as very important. This may, of course, partially reflect a lack of awareness of the number and range of part-time degree courses that are, in fact, available. If this was the case for those who had successfully entered the system, such awareness is presumably much lower for those who have not. The fact that 32 per cent of the students regarded lack of publicity about the courses as a 'very important' barrier lends some support to this interpretation.

Table 4.6   Student perceptions of barriers to access: Factors rated as 'very important'.

Barriers	%
Lack of availability of suitable part-time degree courses at a reasonable distance	54
Lack of necessary educational qualifications	34
Lack of awareness by colleges of the special needs of part-time students	32
Lack of publicity about the availability of such courses	32
Financial costs	28
Uncertainty about the academic level of degree studies	27
Lack of self-confidence of potential students	22
Lack of provision by colleges of preparatory back-to-study courses	19

Over one-third of the students cited lack of educational qualifications as a very important barrier. There has been some discussion recently about the limited use made by courses of the opportunities to enrol students with non-standard entry qualifications (see Evans, 1984) and, in particular, to give credit for experiential learning in entry criteria. Even if courses are enabled to make more use of these opportunities, there will still be a need for a greater awareness of this by students and potential students.

Attitudes of others towards part-time study

The questionnaire asked about the attitudes of other people who might have a significant effect upon the students in the sample. In computing the percentages shown in Table 4.7, the 'not applicable' responses were first deleted.

It is clear from Table 4.7 that little discouragement from any of the above sources was reported. Most encouragement was drawn from the students' family and the other members of the course (staff and fellow students). Work (employers and colleagues) provided a supportive environment for about two-thirds of the sample. For a majority of the respondents, friends outside of work were seen as having a neutral impact on their motivation.

It is likely that the results shown in Table 4.7 reflect the sources of encouragement actually sought by students. Most married students, for example, are presumably aware of the need to secure the support of their spouse in view of the impact of undertaking part-time degree level study on domestic arrangements and responsibilities. Course teams might reflect on how students might be encouraged to widen the base of their support to include less obvious people who are influential in their lives, such as friends outside of work.

Table 4.7 Attitudes of others towards part-time courses of study.

	Very supportive (%)	Generally supportive (%)	Neutral/ no effect (%)	Discouraging or opposed (%)
Spouse/partner	63	28	5	3
Other members of your family	37	41	21	2
College staff	34	53	13	0[a]
Fellow students	33	48	19	0[a]
Your employer	27	41	27	5
People who you work with	16	45	34	4
Friends outside of work	11	35	52	2

Note: Horizontal percentages sum to 100 per cent.
[a] Less than 0.5 per cent.

Choice of particular course

Sometimes, students have a choice between a part-time degree course at more than one institution or whether to pursue a full-time degree course, often they have a choice of whether to undertake a non-degree course and always they have a choice of whether to undertake a course at all. The issue of the choice between an Open University degree course and a polytechnic or college part-time degree course is examined later. This section looks more generally at factors influencing student choice of the particular course at the particular institution where they were enrolled.

Table 4.8 Importance attached to various factors in choice of present course.

Factors	Very important (%)	Fairly important (%)	Unimportant (%)
Practical factors			
I could study without giving up my present job/career	93	5	2
The pattern of attendance fitted in with my domestic responsibilities	55	28	18
It was near where I live/work	45	35	21
I could get on the course despite my lack of qualifications	31	21	48
It allowed me to vary the pace of my studies	26	38	35
Features of the course itself			
The level of the qualification offered	76	20	4
The broad subject of the degree	46	42	13
The particular subjects available within the course	45	44	11
The amount of required class attendance	31	43	25
The course structure	23	52	25
The teaching methods	19	49	31
The level of course fees	17	25	58
The amount of required private study	17	47	37
The assessment methods	14	46	40
Other factors			
I could get exemption from part of the course	31	24	46
Employer encouraged me to take this course	30	38	32
It was recommended by others, e.g. students/friends	14	47	39
Spouse, friends, etc., were already taking this course	8	31	61

Note: Horizontal percentages sum to 100 per cent.

The questionnaire presented a list of factors grouped under the headings 'features of the course itself', 'practical factors' and 'other factors', and asked respondents to say how important each was in choosing their present course. The questionnaire allowed students to respond 'not applicable' and these responses were excluded before the percentages in Table 4.8 were computed.

The two factors that were considered to be 'very important' by more than 75 per cent of the respondents were being able to study without giving up their present job/career and the level of the qualification offered. The factors considered as 'very important' by about half of the respondents were that the course fitted in with domestic responsibilities, its proximity to the student's home or work and the subject matter of the course. Compared to these factors, more academic matters such as the teaching methods and assessment methods were perceived as of much more modest importance.

If one is looking for one simple message from Table 4.8, it is that improving the attractiveness and general level of enrolments on part-time degree courses is firstly a matter of making them more widely available (and one might add, in the light of previous sections of this report, making them more widely known) in a wide range of subjects and only secondarily a matter of achieving excellence in terms of course content.

Choice between a CNAA part-time degree course and an Open University course

This section looks at the reasons why students chose a CNAA part-time degree course as opposed to an Open University degree course. The questionnaire presented the respondents with a list of possible factors and invited them to

Table 4.9   Reasons for choosing a CNAA rather than an Open University course.

Reason	%
Preferred course with face-to-face tuition	78
More contact with tutors	65
More contact with fellow students	59
Availability of on-site facilities (library, computer, etc.)	52
Didn't consider an Open University course	38
Less self-discipline needed than for distance learning with Open University	33
CNAA course had a better reputation/recommended	26
Previous study at this college	21
Employer encouraged me to take this CNAA course	20
Open University didn't offer a degree in the subject that I wished to study	18
Lower cost than Open University course	16
Couldn't get a place on an Open University course	1

indicate as many as applied to themselves (Table 4.9). Most of the respondents gave several reasons for preferring a CNAA part-time degree course.

The reason that was most frequently mentioned (by almost 80 per cent of the respondents) was face-to-face tuition. This was also the reason the largest number of the respondents reported as being the 'most important'. This result presumably reflects the fact that preferred learning style varies across the population. It emphasizes the importance of making higher education available in a variety of modes of delivery. For these students, the attractions of distance learning are clearly very limited. This does not rule out the possibility of some *optional* distance learning units on part-time degree courses outside of the Open University, but it does suggest that the scope for fundamental innovations in this area is probably not large.

The next most popular responses were greater contact with staff and fellow students. Such contact is presumably important for academic support and feedback on progress. These responses also suggest that there is an important social dimension to the educational experience of these part-time students. Those who are responsible for operating part-time degree courses might wish to reflect upon how this can be developed to enhance the learning experience and the likelihood of successful completion.

For over 50 per cent of the respondents, the availability of on-site facilities (library, computers, etc.) was an important reason. College authorities might bear this in mind when they are making decisions about college facilities that will affect part-time students.

A total of 38 per cent claim not to have considered an Open University course. This is a disturbingly high figure and one might have hoped that all applicants to CNAA part-time degree courses would be encouraged to consider the alternatives in order to identify the course of higher education that most meets their needs. An admissions interview is an appropriate place for this sort of educational counselling. One-third of the students perceived the self-discipline needed for distance learning to be a disincentive to undertaking an Open University course. These students apparently valued the rhythm and ritual of regular class attendance.

Over one-quarter (26 per cent) mentioned that they preferred the CNAA part-time course because it had been recommended or because of its reputation. Remember that, in terms of students enrolled on part-time degree programmes more generally, the respondents to this questionnaire were a biased sample – they were the ones who had chosen CNAA courses. No doubt a sizeable proportion of those enrolled with the Open University would have given the same reason for choosing an Open University course.

'Previous study at this college' was a reason given by 21 per cent of the respondents. This emphasizes the value of maintaining part-time sub-degree work as a factor affecting the recruitment to degree level courses. A total of 20 per cent of the respondents were encouraged to take their CNAA part-time degree course by their employer. In the light of the significant assistance given to part-time students by their employer, this would have been an important consideration.

In view of the very different distribution of subjects offered by the Open University from those that are available as CNAA part-time degree courses, the proportion of respondents who claimed that a reason for their preference was because the 'Open University didn't offer a degree in the subject that I wished to study' was surprisingly small at only 18 per cent. It is also surprising that only 16 per cent mentioned the higher cost of Open University courses. The only reason that was mentioned by fewer respondents (1 per cent) was the inability to get a place on an Open University course. It would appear that students who are unable to gain admission to an Open University course do not, for the most part, end up on a CNAA part-time degree course. It would be interesting to know if the converse is also the case.

'Other' reasons that were mentioned by the respondents included the fact that on CNAA degree courses the times of the terms are similar to school terms, which is convenient for those with children. Also, there was a perception among some students that Open University degree courses take longer.

Summary

1. *Main aim.* The improvement of career prospects was by far the most important aim reported by the respondents to the questionnaire. It was selected as the 'main aim' by more than three times the number of respondents who selected the next most popular main aim (which was 'to prove to myself or others that I could complete a degree course'). Over three-quarters of the respondents rated 'to improve my career prospects' as a 'very important' aim. As a broad generalization, work-related aims were regarded as most important followed by personal development aims and subject-related aims, with other aims as least important.

Almost half of the respondents reported that they will use their degree qualification to 'join, obtain exemption from or gain higher status in a professional body' relevant to their career/occupation. A total of 40 per cent envisaged undertaking further study for the examinations of a professional body.

2. *Academic aims.* A substantial proportion of the respondents envisaged higher level academic study: 35 per cent in the case of taught Master's degrees and 23 per cent in the case of research degrees. A *majority* of respondents expressed positive interest in proceeding to further part-time study for a higher level academic award in a similar field of study if this were possible at the college at which they were currently enrolled.

3. *Information.* Among the respondents to the questionnaire, the single most common first source of information about their part-time degree courses was the college prospectus. Presumably, most of these would have been student-initiated enquiries. Of the formal information channels, only the local press accounted for a substantial percentage of responses. Information about the

availability of part-time degree courses seems to be heavily dependent upon the efficacy of informal channels (such as colleagues at work). With the expansion of part-time degree course provision over the last 10 years, it is possible that the time is now right for a national (or at least regional) initiative in disseminating information to provide a more general awareness to facilitate the local efforts of course leaders.

Only about 25 per cent of the respondents were aware of the existence of their course for more than 2 years prior to enrolment. This would appear to be further evidence of a lack of general awareness of the availability of part-time degree courses within polytechnics and other colleges of higher education.

4. *Barriers to access*. The questionnaire sought the views of part-time students on potential barriers to access to part-time degree courses. 'Lack of availability of suitable part-time degree courses at a reasonable distance' was regarded as the most important barrier. This may, of course, partially reflect a lack of awareness of the number and range of part-time degree courses that are in fact available.

Little discouragement from taking a part-time degree course was reported. Most encouragement was drawn from the students' families and other members of the course (staff and fellow students).

5. *Choices*. The question on the reasons for choice of a particular course at a particular institution produced responses that focused on the practical rather than the academic. This suggested the following broad generalization: improving the attractiveness and general level of enrolments on part-time degree courses is firstly a matter of making them more widely available and more widely known and only then a matter of achieving excellence in terms of course content.

The most frequently mentioned reason for choosing a CNAA part-time degree course rather than an Open University course (by almost 80 per cent of the respondents) was face-to-face tuition. This was also the reason the largest number of respondents reported as 'most important'. The next most popular responses were greater contact with staff and fellow students. For 50 per cent of the respondents, the availability of on-site facilities (libraries, computers, etc.) was an important reason.

A total of 38 per cent claim not to have considered an Open University course. This is a disturbingly high figure and one might have hoped that all applicants to CNAA part-time degree courses would be encouraged to consider the alternatives in order to identify the course of higher education that most meets their needs. Only 16 per cent mentioned the higher cost of Open University courses. Less than 1 per cent mentioned an inability to get a place on an Open University course.

5 | The Students' Experiences

This chapter looks at some of the experiences of the students on their CNAA part-time degree courses. Further analysis and discussion of student attitudes to their experiences and the difficulties that they encountered can be found in the following chapters. This chapter starts at the point at which most students make their first face-to-face contact with the course: at an interview for admission to the course.

Entry to the course

Interviews

Of those who responded to the survey, 71 per cent attended an interview for their course. It is common practice for part-time degree courses to use interviews as a means of providing information *to* the candidate as well as obtaining information *from* the candidate. The interview can take the form of educational counselling, in which the needs of the candidate are explored to assess whether the course is the most appropriate one to meet those needs. An interview of this kind would seem to be a simple way of reducing unnecessary non-completion by students. In view of this, it may seem surprising that 29 per cent of the respondents attended no interview and it is difficult to resist the feeling that some courses are losing an opportunity here.

Pre-course information

Students might reasonably expect to receive full and accurate information about the course on which they are enrolling and the majority of respondents felt that they had. The questionnaire asked: 'How different (if at all) is the content of your course from what you expected when you enrolled?' Of the respondents, 5 per cent said that it was 'significantly different', 24 per cent said that it was 'quite different' and 71 per cent (a similar percentage to those who had attended admissions interviews) said that it was 'not significantly different'.

Table 5.1 Satisfaction with pre-course information.

	Very good or fairly good (%)	Adequate (%)	Very poor or fairly poor (%)
Amount of required class attendance	73	23	5
Financial costs	63	28	9
Course structure	58	32	10
Course content	57	30	12
Amount of required private study	49	34	18
Academic difficulty of course	46	38	15
Teaching methods	40	40	20

Note: Horizontal percentages sum to 100.

The respondents were then presented with a list of seven specific factors and were asked to express their level of satisfaction with the information that they received before starting the course (Table 5.1). Clearly, it is easier to provide information to students on some matters than on others. Informing students of the amount of required class attendance is not difficult. Providing information on the academic difficulty of a course is much less easy. It should, however, be possible to give students a reasonable appreciation of the teaching methods that will be employed and it should be possible in an interview situation to provide a fair indication of the amount of required private study. In fact, this is just the sort of information that is most effectively conveyed in an interview.

Finally, on the subject of pre-course information, the students were asked to give an overall assessment. A total of 60 per cent of the respondents reported that the information that they received before starting their course was either 'very good' or 'fairly good'. A further 32 per cent found it 'adequate'. Readers can make their own assessment of whether this represents a satisfactory level of achievement by courses. Course management teams might wish to investigate the level of satisfaction of students on their own courses and make comparisons with these figures.

Entry tests

Few courses administer any form of test of written or quantitative skills to candidates for admission. Only 8 per cent of the respondents encountered such a test. In view of the relatively high level of educational qualifications of those entering part-time CNAA degree courses, this is perhaps not surprising. Some courses might consider the value of such tests combined with less demanding requirements in terms of conventional entry qualifications. Until effective methods of evaluating experiential learning have been identified (the objective of another project sponsored by CNAA Development Services), this could provide a more flexible admissions policy while still preserving the security required by some courses.

Study skills

Many of the students have not engaged in formal study for many years when they first start their part-time degree courses. Most have not had previous experience of degree level study. The study skills of the students are likely to be rusty and very limited for the purposes of part-time study at an advanced level.

Asked whether they had received any guidance on study skills when they started their courses, 36 per cent of the respondents gave affirmative responses. This means, of course, that almost two-thirds were not aware of receiving any study skills guidance at the outset of their courses. This does not preclude the possibility that guidance on study skills is integrated into the various course units without being explicitly identified as such.

Some would argue that the subject content of the learning is subordinate to fostering the continuing process of learning (see Rogers, 1983). One does not have to go this far to agree that helping students to learn how to learn more effectively is an important objective for courses of education at all levels. Facts become outdated, but learning how to learn more effectively benefits students for the rest of their lives. The development of study skills is one significant element of this.

There does seem to be a strong case for explicitly addressing the issue of study skills at the outset of part-time degree courses. For one such course (and there may be others), study skills provides the focus of a residential weekend for new students. This also, of course, helps to develop social cohesiveness among the students, which has additional educational benefits. Course management teams might wish to consider this as an example of good practice.

Table 5.2   Number of hours
of course attendance per week.

Hours	%
4 or less	6
5	11
6	37
7	4
8	3
9	13
10	9
11	7
12	7
Over 12	4
Total	101

Table 5.3 Number of hours of course attendance per week by subject group.

Hours	Engineering/ technology (%)	Sciences (%)	Arts/ humanities (%)	Social sciences (%)	Business studies (%)	Education (%)
4 or less	0	3	3	3	5	30
5	0	1	4	21	21	24
6	1	10	60	62	69	41
7	2	4	5	6	2	3
8	5	4	8	2	1	1
9	16	37	6	5	1	0
10	27	11	7	0	0	0
11	21	8	5	0	0	0
12	17	16	1	0	0	0
Over 12	12	7	1	0	0	0
Total	101	101	100	99	99	99
Median	10	9	6	6	6	6
Mean	10.6	9.5	7.0	6.0	5.8	5.1

Teaching and learning methods

Weekly hours of attendance

The average (median) number of hours of required course attendance per week was 6, but there was substantial variation across courses (Table 5.2). A substantial part of this variation can be explained by differences between subject areas (Table 5.3). The average weekly hours of course attendance is highest for the engineering/technology subject group, followed by the science subjects. Arts/humanities, social sciences and business studies are closely grouped around 6 hours per week. Education has a higher proportion of students on courses with fewer required hours of attendance.

Private study

The average number of hours per week that the respondents spent studying in addition to attending classes was 9 (Table 5.4). Adding the average hours of classroom attendance for the respondents to that for private study, gives an average (mean) of 16.7 hours per week for study on their part-time degree courses.

There was an inverse correlation in the data between the weekly hours of class attendance and hours of private study. One might infer from this that for some courses private study is the principal learning vehicle, with classes providing guidance and a forum for reflecting on the results, whereas for other courses the classroom is the focus for learning activities.

Most of the respondents (78 per cent) were satisfied with the balance between class attendance and private study. Of those that were not satisfied, a larger

Table 5.4 Average number of hours of private study per week.

Hours	%
1–3	10
4–6	33
7–9	15
10–12	24
13–15	9
16–18	3
19–21	3
Over 21	3
Total	100

Table 5.5 Student preferences: Class attendance and private study.

Preference	%
Would prefer more class attendance and less private study	15
Would prefer more private study and less class attendance	7
Neither of the above – the present balance is about right	78
Total	100

percentage would prefer a shift in the balance towards more class attendance (Table 5.5).

Incidence of lectures

As with total hours of attendance, there was wide variation in the weekly number of hours of formal lectures (Table 5.6). The subject distribution of formal lecture hours was similar to that for the distribution of total hours of attendance. In general, subjects that require high numbers of hours of attendance tend to use a high proportion of those hours for formal lectures.

Given the high proportion of student class contact that is accounted for by formal lectures, it is interesting to note students' preferences on this issue. Nine per cent of the respondents wanted more lectures and less of other forms of class contact compared with 15 per cent who wanted less lectures and more of other forms of class contact. The remainder thought their current balance about right (Table 5.7).

Table 5.6 Number of hours of lectures per week.

Hours	%
2 or less	6
3	15
4	14
5	16
6	19
7	8
8	7
9	8
10 or more	6
Total	99

Table 5.7   Student preferences: Formal lectures and other forms of class contact.

Preference	%
Would prefer more formal lectures and less of other forms of class contact	9
Would prefer less formal lectures and more of other forms of class contact	15
Neither of the above – the present balance is about right	77
Total	100

Other learning activities

Overall, about 75 per cent of the class contact of the respondents took the form of formal lectures. One might reasonably wonder whether such a high proportion is altogether desirable. Professional students of education would probably say not. For the respondents, lectures were perceived as being very helpful but not especially enjoyable. The survey questionnaire presented students with a list of learning activities that they might have encountered on their courses and asked them to rate them as 'very enjoyable', 'fairly enjoyable' or 'not enjoyable'. They were also asked to rate them as 'very helpful', 'fairly helpful' or 'not helpful'. It is appreciated that some of the learning activities would not have been present on some of the courses and the questionnaire provided a 'not applicable/too early to say' option for each learning activity. The latter responses were excluded before the percentages shown in Tables 5.8 and 5.9 were computed so the results pertain only to those who were able (and willing) to rate each learning activity. A good appreciation of the results can be obtained by focusing on the 'very enjoyable' and 'very helpful' responses.

Table 5.8   Learning activities rated 'very enjoyable' (percentage of applicable responses).

Learning activity	%
Practical work	40
Use of computer	40
Small group work with tutor present	35
Independent work (e.g. project work)	27
Small group work without tutor present	25
Lectures	23
Private study (e.g. course reading)	16
Quantitative work	13
Programmed learning	10
Preparation of written work	8

Table 5.9   Learning activities rated 'very helpful' (percentage of applicable responses).

Learning activity	%
Lectures	56
Small group work with tutor present	46
Private study (e.g. course reading)	42
Independent work (e.g. project work)	40
Practical work	34
Preparation of written work	33
Use of computer	31
Small group work without tutor present	18
Quantitative work	14
Programmed learning	10

There might be a suspicion in these results that some students perceive the word 'helpful' narrowly in terms of examination success. Lectures and preparation of written work are activities that are seen as helpful though not particularly enjoyable. Practical work is popular but ranks less highly in terms of helpfulness. Small group work with a tutor present (for the most part, presumably, seminars and tutorials) and independent work (e.g. project work) rank high on both scales. The students appear to find programmed learning both unpleasant and unhelpful. It would appear that distance learning based on programmed instruction would not find much support among these students!

Number of concurrent courses

The average (median) number of different subjects that respondents were currently studying was three. Once again, however, there was a sizeable dispersion (Table 5.10). One wonders whether there was some misunderstanding of the word 'subject' in the survey question ('How many different subjects

Table 5.10   Number of concurrent subjects.

No.	%
1	6
2	20
3	38
4	15
5	8
6	7
More than 6	7
Total	101

are you currently studying at the same time on your course?') that produced these responses. Some difficulty was experienced in designing this question to ensure that the meaning would be clear to the respondents. Can there really be part-time students carrying more than six different subjects at the same time? Whether or not the question was ambiguous, the responses prompt the question: Would it not be better, in some cases, to teach fewer subjects in parallel and teach more subjects in series? For example, instead of teaching four subjects in parallel over a whole year, perhaps it would be worth considering the desirability of teaching two subjects more intensively for one semester each. By reducing the range of subjects with which the student must cope at any one time, workloads would be more manageable, examinations would be staggered, thereby reducing the amplitude of examination pressures, and it would also provide more entry points to the course – permitting more flexibility for exemptions. There have been some experiments with 'intensive teaching' (see, for example, Parlett and King, 1971) and part-time degree courses might be a fruitful field in which to apply the results.

Distance learning units

One major distinction between CNAA part-time degree courses and Open University courses is that the former involve substantial class attendance, whereas the latter are, for the most part, based on distance learning. Indeed, face-to-face tuition and more contact with tutors were the reasons most frequently cited by the respondents for choosing CNAA part-time programmes. However, it is plausible that this dichotomy has been drawn too tightly and that there is scope for introducing some distance learning elements into CNAA undergraduate courses. In order to test the attractiveness of this proposal, the students were asked whether they would be interested in completing one or more course units by means of distance learning. The response was mixed (Table 5.11).

Half of the respondents did not favour this idea. The other half expressed some level of positive interest (13 per cent gave the 'definitely' response). On the basis of these results, there would seem to be a case for some experimentation with this idea, but it would appear to be better to offer it as an *option* rather than

Table 5.11   Interest in undertaking distance learning units.

Response	%
Definitely	13
Probably	14
Possibly	23
Definitely not or probably not	50
Total	100

Table 5.12 Proportion of assessment accounted for by course-work.

% of coursework	% of respondents
0–10	16
11–20	18
21–30	27
31–40	16
41–50	11
Over 50	12
Total	100

Mean = 30 per cent
Median = 33 per cent

as a *replacement* for some face-to-face tuition. Some, of the students at least, would appreciate greater freedom to choose.

The role of coursework in assessment

Coursework is used as a means of assessment on most of the courses in addition to its use as part of the learning process. Its incidence in assessment among the survey respondents is shown in Table 5.12. There is clearly wide variation in the extent to which coursework contributes to student assessment. A total of 95 per cent of the respondents wanted its current level of contribution to be maintained or increased (Table 5.13).

College support for students

Chapter 3 looked at evidence of support for part-time degree students in terms of institutional facilities using information drawn from a questionnaire sent to course leaders. The aim of this section is much more modest: to collate together some results from the student survey which contained questions that pertain to

Table 5.13 Coursework: Student preferences.

	%
Would prefer coursework to have a smaller role in assessment	5
Would prefer coursework to have a larger role in assessment	52
Neither of the above – the present balance is about right	43
Total	100

academic support, personal tutoring facilities and support from the students' union.

Academic support

Part-time undergraduates sometimes have to miss classes due to unforeseen domestic or work commitments. Some courses have a policy of ensuring that, for each subject, the students receive at the beginning of each academic session a list of topics that will be covered each week with references to appropriate readings. This is designed to ensure that the student who is unable to attend classes for a week is not too disadvantaged. It is clearly beneficial also to the students who do not have to miss classes as it enables them to be able to plan their studies more effectively and take more responsibility for their own learning. The students in the survey were asked: 'If you are unable to attend classes for a week, do you have enough course information to enable you to maintain the continuity of your studies by private study?' A total of 85 per cent of the respondents reported that, for some subjects at least, the course provides academic support for students subject to unavoidable absences. The remaining 15 per cent gives cause for concern. The practice of providing a detailed programme (including appropriate readings) identifying the ground that will be covered each week of a course is recommended.

The responses also suggest that where courses have a policy of providing the sort of support outlined above, there is substantial variation in its implementation. Less than half of the respondents were receiving this sort of academic support in all the subjects that they were currently studying: it would appear that on some courses it is left up to individual members of the teaching staff, whereas on others course management teams seem to be more effective in monitoring its implementation.

Personal tutors

Eighty per cent of the respondents claimed to have a personal tutor on their course 'from whom they could seek advice about difficulties'. The remaining 20 per cent presumably had no personal tutor, were unaware of having a personal tutor or had a personal tutor from whom they did not feel that they could seek advice about difficulties.

Views may differ on the importance of personal tutors for part-time students compared to their full-time counterparts. On the one hand, it may be argued that the need is greater for full-time students, most of whom are young and living away from home for the first time, than for mature part-time students. In other words, the very maturity of part-time mature students diminishes the need. On the other hand, it may be argued that the long gap experienced by many part-time students between previous academic experience and the additional domestic and work commitments and pressures makes the need greater.

Probably the safest conclusion is that the needs of part-time and full-time students are simply different in terms of personal tutoring. On small, part-time courses, it may be sufficient if the students feel that they can discuss problems with their course leader or year tutor. It would seem to be essential, however, that there is some member of course staff who can respond to student problems if only to ensure that the problems are, where appropriate, brought to the attention of the relevant examinations board.

Students' unions

The questionnaire asked respondents 'Are you a member of the students' union at your college?' A total of 35 per cent said 'yes', 57 per cent said 'no' and the remaining 8 per cent recorded 'don't know'. Therefore, almost two-thirds of the respondents either believed that they were not members of the student union at their college or they did not know whether they were or not. While union membership may not be automatic for part-time students at some institutions, the conclusion that could be drawn from this finding is that student unions are failing to meet the needs of part-time students. Part-time students clearly have less time to become engaged in student union activities and politics, but these results suggest that student unions should ask themselves (or be asked) what responsibility they have to part-time students and whether this substantial proportion of their constituency is being neglected.

Summary

1. *Applications and admissions.* Most (71 per cent) of the survey's respondents attended an interview for their course. Few courses administer any form of test of written or quantitative skills to candidates for admission. Only 8 per cent of the respondents encountered such a test. Some courses might consider the value of such tests, combined with less demanding entry requirements in terms of conventional entry qualifications.

Sixty per cent of the respondents regarded the information that they received before starting their course as 'very good' or 'fairly good'. Almost 10 per cent regarded it as 'fairly poor' or 'very poor'. Almost two-thirds of the respondents were unaware of having received guidance on study skills when they started their courses. There certainly seems to be a case for addressing this issue at the outset of part-time degree courses.

2. *Hours of attendance and private study.* The average (median) number of hours of required course attendance per week was 6 (mean = 7.7), and the average number of additional hours per week that the respondents spent in private study was 9. Almost 80 per cent of the respondents were satisfied with the balance between class attendance and private study. Of the remainder, most would prefer a shift in the balance towards more class attendance.

There was a wide variation in the number of hours per week spent in formal lectures. Overall, about three-quarters of the class contact of the respondents took the form of lectures. Over three-quarters of the respondents thought that the present balance between lectures and other forms of class contact was 'about right'. Of the remainder, most would prefer a shift in the balance towards fewer formal lectures. Small groupwork with a tutor present and independent work (e.g. project work) was regarded as both helpful and enjoyable. Lectures and preparation of written work was perceived as helpful though not especially enjoyable. Practical work was popular but ranked less highly in terms of helpfulness. Only a small percentage of the students regarded programmed learning as either enjoyable or helpful.

3. *Subject loading.* The average (median) number of different subjects that the respondents were currently studying was three, but there were some examples of students carrying six or more subjects at the same time. This prompts the question of whether 'intensive teaching' of fewer subjects over shorter time periods has a contribution to make to part-time degree courses.

4. *Distance learning.* Half of the students expressed some level of positive interest in the possibility of studying some course units by distance learning. This implies, of course, that the idea was unattractive to the other half of the respondents. There would appear to be a case for some experimentation with this idea, but as an option rather than as a requirement as a compulsory replacement for some face-to-face tuition.

5. *Assessment.* On average, coursework accounted for almost 30 per cent of the total student assessment. A majority (52 per cent) of the respondents would prefer coursework to play a larger role in assessment and only 5 per cent would prefer it to play a smaller role in assessment.

6. *Academic and other support.* A total of 47 per cent of the respondents reported that for all subjects the course provides academic support for students subject to unavoidable absences, 38 per cent reported such support for some subjects, only leaving 15 per cent without any such support. Eighty per cent of the respondents had a personal tutor 'from whom they could seek advice about difficulties'. Almost two-thirds of the respondents either believed that they were not members of the student union at their college or didn't know whether they were or not.

6 | Student Assessment of the Courses and Student Difficulties

This chapter is mostly concerned with the difficulties encountered by under-graduates enrolled on part-time courses accredited by the CNAA. First, however, some consideration is given to student assessment of their courses.

Student assessment of courses

The questionnaire contained a number of questions that were designed to provide an indication of the general level of student satisfaction with their courses. Satisfaction is, of course, related to expectations, and therefore some of the questions sought to compare student perceptions of the actuality with their level of initial expectations. For over 90 per cent of the respondents, their course had at least 'lived up to their expectations' (Table 6.1). These will be reassuring findings for those staff in the colleges who are responsible for developing, administering and teaching on part-time undergraduate programmes.

A further indication of the levels of satisfaction felt by the students is obtained by the responses to the question 'Would you recommend this course to a friend in a similar position to yourself when you started?' – 89 per cent answered 'yes'. Courses with low levels of recruitment might care to bear this result in mind. The existing students and graduates are potentially powerful agents for recruitment.

The questionnaire asked: 'Have the benefits overall of taking the course *so far* been greater or less than you expected when you decided to enrol?' For

Table 6.1 Student overall assessment of courses.

Assessment	%
Roughly as expected	72
Better than expected	20
Worse than expected	8
Total	100

Table 6.2   Perceived future benefits from completing course.

Assessment	%
Roughly as expected	62
Greater benefits than originally expected	27
Not as great as expected	11
Total	100

two-thirds of the respondents, the benefits were 'roughly as expected'. As for the others, 25 per cent responded 'more than expected' and only 8 per cent responded 'less than expected'.

The final question concerned with overall student satisfaction asked: 'Compared with when you decided to enrol on the course, do you now expect the eventual benefits from completing the course to be greater or less?' The responses to this question would, of course, depend upon changes in the circumstances of the students as well as their evaluation of the course *per se*. For example, it is clear that career-related aims were important for a high percentage of the students, so that changes in a student's employment circumstances (such as a move to or from an employment in which the possession of a degree increased promotion opportunities) could affect the perceived value of completing the course. The responses to this question are shown in Table 6.2.

The overall impression gained from the responses to these questions is that for about two-thirds of the students, the courses were generally living up to their expectations, for about one-quarter of the students the courses exceeded their expectations, and about 10 per cent were disappointed.

When the students were presented with a list of specific college- and course-related factors, the reactions were much more mixed (Table 6.3). The responses indicating that a factor was 'not applicable' were excluded before the percentages were computed. At the most general level, these results suggest a higher level of overall satisfaction with the courses as such than with the college facilities.

Looking first at the various dimensions of the courses, it can be seen that very high levels of satisfaction were expressed by the respondents regarding relationships between staff and students, course content and the helpfulness of the staff. It is possible that the staff who become involved with developing and teaching on part-time courses are a particularly committed band of lecturers. Because the material rewards of so doing at the personal and departmental level are limited (see Bourner, 1983), it may be that job satisfaction is the principal incentive and that this is reflected in the favourable responses of the students.

The dimensions of the courses which afforded least satisfaction were the arrangements for students to make their voices heard in course evaluation, feedback to students on their performance and progress and opportunities to vary the pace of their studies. These are issues to which course management teams might profitably direct their attention in course design, monitoring and evaluation.

The respondents expressed high levels of satisfaction with library opening hours and loan regulations, but rather less satisfaction with the availability of

Table 6.3 Level of satisfaction with aspects of course and college.

	Very or fairly satisfactory (%)	Fairly unsatisfactory (%)	Very unsatisfactory (%)
The course			
Relationships between staff and students	97	3	1
Helpfulness of staff	95	4	1
Content of course	95	4	1
Teaching methods	88	10	3
Appreciation by staff of difficulties of part-time study	84	13	3
Course administration	82	14	4
Arrangements for students to make their voices heard in course evaluation	76	18	6
Feedback to students on performance/progress	65	28	7
Opportunity to vary pace of study:	62	30	8
College facilities			
Library opening hours	88	7	4
Computing facilities	88	9	3
Library loan regulations	87	9	4
Laboratories	86	10	4
Provision of up-to-date equipment	84	12	3
Physical enviroment (e.g. buildings/classrooms)	81	14	5
Availability in library of books and journals recommended by staff	70	18	11
Refectory/canteen facilities	62	21	17
Pre-school childcare facilities (on campus or locally)	22	14	65

Note: Horizontal percentages sum to 100.

books and journals recommended by staff. The latter may reflect cutbacks in library spending in recent years or may simply reflect the fact that the part-time students are disadvantaged in terms of access to library facilities compared to their full-time counterparts. For most of the part-time undergraduate programmes covered in this survey, there are corresponding full-time (or sandwich) courses at the same institutions where the reading lists are presumably fairly similar. It is not unknown for part-time students to complain that by the time that they can get to the libraries, most of the books that they have been recommended have already been borrowed by full-time students. Some libraries address this problem by making special library loan arrangements for part-time students and libraries might wish to compare practices in this area.

The two factors that produced the highest proportions of dissatisfied respondents were refectory facilities and pre-school child-care facilities. The latter is a special case in that this question was only answered by 10 per cent of the respondents (the others indicating that it was not applicable), and for those for whom it was applicable it generated by far the most dissatisfaction. These two facts may, of course, be related. If pre-school child-care facilities are a prerequisite for enrolling on a part-time degree course for some potential students, then their absence would account for the low level of respondents to whom this question was applicable.

Student perceptions of academic level

The questionnaire asked the following question: 'On the whole, do you consider that a CNAA part-time degree is equivalent to a CNAA full-time degree in the same subject? And how do you think others feel about it?' Three-quarters of the part-time students thought that CNAA part-time degree courses are of equivalent standard to CNAA full-time degree courses. Of the remainder, a majority thought that part-time degree courses are of a higher standard (11 versus 7 per cent) (Table 6.4).

The respondents, however, clearly felt less sanguine about the perceptions of others, though not surprisingly the percentage of 'don't knows' increased as the question moved from 'self' to 'your employer' to 'academics in institutions of higher education'. They thought that their employers were less inclined to rate the relative standard of CNAA part-time degree courses as highly as they did themselves: 6 per cent indicating a higher standard and 10 per cent indicating a lower standard. For academics in institutions of higher education, the percentages were 3 per cent (higher standard) versus 26 per cent (lower standard). It would be interesting to discover whether these latter perceptions have any basis in fact. If they do not, it would clearly be valuable to be able to provide the students with reassurance on this matter. This is especially important in view of the substantial percentage of the respondents who wished to use their part-time degree as a basis for further academic study (see Chapter 4).

The questionnaire also contained a question that sought respondents' perceptions of the standard of CNAA part-time degrees compared to Open

Table 6.4 CNAA part-time and full-time degree courses compared.

CNAA part-time degree is:	Self (%)	Your employer[a] (%)	Academics in institutions of higher education (%)
of a higher standard than CNAA full-time degree	11	6	3
equivalent to CNAA full-time degree	75	56	33
of a lower standard than CNAA full-time degree	7	10	26
don't know	7	28	38
Total	100	100	100

[a] Percentage of applicable responses.

University degree courses. The numbers of 'don't knows' were higher in this case (for self, for employer and for academics in institutions of higher education). Very few of those who responded (less than 3 per cent) perceived their CNAA part-time degree as being of a lower standard (for employers and academics in institutions of higher education the corresponding figures were 3 and 5 per cent). Of the others, about half considered their CNAA part-time degree course to be of a higher standard and half considered it to be of equivalent standard. Once again, it should be remembered that, in the context of this question, the respondents represent a biased sample – they were all students who had chosen a CNAA part-time degree course. The perceptions of a sample of students enrolled on Open University courses would, no doubt, be very different.

Difficulties experienced by the students

Despite the higher overall levels of reported satisfaction with the courses, over 30 per cent of the respondents said that they had, at some time, considered leaving their courses before completing them. This finding suggests that they had encountered substantially greater difficulties than they expected when they enrolled. The important problem of non-completion is addressed later in the book. This section, however, sets the scene by looking firstly at the difficulties encountered in relation to difficulties expected at enrolment, and then examining in more detail some specific areas where problems were experienced.

For about three-quarters of the students, the difficulties, overall, had been roughly as expected (Table 6.5). The number of respondents for whom the difficulties were greater than expected exceeded those for whom the difficulties were less than expected by a factor of more than three to one. Only 5 per cent experienced less difficulties overall than expected.

Table 6.5   Difficulties overall compared to expectation at enrolment.

Assessment	%
Roughly as expected	77
More difficult	18
Less difficult	5
Total	100

The admissions interview would seem to be an appropriate vehicle for exploring with the student expected difficulties. Certainly it would seem to be important, at some stage in the admissions process, for staff to emphasize to students the difficulties that they are likely to encounter. Table 6.6 should be helpful to admissions tutors in identifying the areas where unexpectedly severe difficulties are likely to arise. It is important to be clear that Table 6.6 does not indicate the levels of difficulty experienced by the students with the various factors. It compares the difficulties experienced by the students *compared with their initial expectations*. It also indicates how well the students were able to assess the level of difficulty that each of the factors would present.

The items in the 'study and learning difficulties' category will be examined first. Probably the most important result shown is that 54 per cent of the respondents encountered more difficulty finding the time to study than they had expected when they enrolled. According to the findings of the survey, a majority of the students are spending over 18 hours per week on course-related activities (including class attendance, private study and travel time). Those in full-time employment who have not carefully thought through the implications of introducing this level of additional time commitment into their lives, are bound to encounter conflicts and stress. Almost 40 per cent of the respondents perceived this as a problem of time management ('organizing my time in an efficient way'). For others, it may be a question of being made more aware of the required level of weekly time commitment necessary to complete their course and being encouraged to work carefully through their priorities to discover where the time can be found. An admissions interview would appear to be an appropriate place to start this process, and it would seem sensible to spend some part of any induction programme addressing this issue.

Developing appropriate study skills and coping with the stress of examinations proved more difficult than expected for more than 20 per cent of the respondents. At least one course known to the authors starts with a weekend residential for new students orientated towards developing study skills (including a time management component), and also has a Saturday morning workshop on 'coping with examinations' about a month before the students take their first examinations. Other courses might wish to consider following this example. Some staff involved in operating part-time degree courses may, as subject specialists, not feel confident about facilitating such workshops. In such cases, they might consider using the available videos that address these issues and they

Table 6.6 Difficulties compared to expectations at enrolment: Specific factors.

	More difficult (%)	Roughly as expected (%)	Less difficult (%)
Study and learning difficulties			
Finding the time to study	54	43	3
Organizing my time in an efficient way	39	54	7
Coping with the stress of examinations	23	63	13
Developing appropriate study skills (e.g. preparation and writing of essays)	23	64	14
Getting used to subjects not previously studied	18	64	18
Remembering important parts of my course	16	73	11
Keeping up with the academic level of the course	16	72	12
Being able to grasp the meaning of specialized terms and concepts	16	71	14
Developing confidence in my academic ability	15	67	18
Coming to terms with the academic way of looking at things	15	67	17
Getting used to a different approach to learning	10	70	21
Getting used to the college environment	2	66	32
Personal, family and job commitments			
Coping with competing demands of hobbies or other interests	43	47	10
Coping with job demands	38	57	6
Coping with family commitments	30	63	7
Coping with the financial costs of the course	16	65	19
Coping with travel to and from college	16	66	18
Coming to terms with changing beliefs and attitudes	7	73	21
Making friends with fellow students	4	66	30

Note: Horizontal percentages sum to 100.

might also consider what help can be sought within their institution from their own educational development units, counselling support services or departments of education.

For some of the items in the 'study and learning difficulties' category, the proportion of the respondents that experienced less difficulty than expected was larger than the proportion that experienced more difficulty than expected. These included getting used to the college environment, a different approach to learning and the academic way of looking at things and also developing confidence in academic ability.

Within the second group of factors in Table 6.6 ('personal, family and job commitments'), the competing demands of family, job and 'other interests' proved more difficult than expected for at least 30 per cent of the respondents. It is possible that these difficulties were largely a result of unexpectedly high demands on the students' time from these sources – lending weight to the comments about time management made above. Two other factors produced more difficulties than expected for over 15 per cent of the respondents: coping with the financial costs and coping with travel to and from college. These issues are explored below.

The changes in a student's circumstances while enrolled on a course may account for some of the unexpected difficulties. The respondents were presented with a list of possible factors that could have an impact and were asked to identify those where changes had increased difficulties in pursuing their course (Table 6.7). Almost 40 per cent of the respondents reported that a change in their job responsibilities had increased their difficulties in pursuing their part-time undergraduate studies. Fourteen per cent identified specifically a change in job location. Because those that mentioned a change of employer or redundancy/unemployment were relatively few (8 and 3 per cent, respectively), it can be inferred that most of the difficulties were produced by changes in current employment. As a majority of the respondents were aged in their late 20s, were upwardly mobile in socio-economic terms and saw career objectives as important in pursuing their studies, it may also be inferred that promotion at work accounted for a significant proportion of the changes in job responsi-

Table 6.7   Changes in personal circumstances that increased difficulties.

	% of respondents
Change in job responsibilities	39
Change in family responsibilities	19
Change of address	18
Change in location of job	14
Change in marital status	9
Change of employer	8
Change in your state of health	7
Redundancy/unemployment	3

bilities. It is possible to envisage a situation of some irony whereby a student's degree studies contributes to promotion that raises the level of work commitments to a point where a student is unable to complete the degree course.

Changes in family responsibilities accounted for increased difficulties for almost 20 per cent of the respondents. One message from this finding is that it is important that the level of commitment required by part-time undergraduate studies be appreciated not only by potential students but also by their families. Applicants should be encouraged at the time of the admissions interview to discuss this issue fully with their family to ensure that it really is appreciated.

The other major item causing greater difficulties than expected was a change of address. Those who have not moved house before are often surprised at the stress and personal disruption that it causes.

It is clear from Table 6.7 that part-time students are vulnerable to a range of factors that are likely to disturb the momentum of their studies. They presumably contribute to student non-completion. The obvious question that this raises is what, if anything, can the college staff do about it.

The issue of providing academic support for students to facilitate the continuity of their studies during periods of unavoidable absence is addressed in Chapter 5. Apart from this, it would seem to be important that students should have some member of staff (whether personal tutor or not) on their courses with whom they can discuss such disruptions to their studies if only because they are the legitimate concern of examination boards. More positively, it is proposed that students could be encouraged to form self-help groups to provide mutual support at such times. Finally, it is suggested that part-time students could make more use of their college's student counselling service. The results of the survey suggest that student counsellors could play a significant role and it is possible that at some colleges they are not always available at times that are appropriate for part-time students. It would not be too radical to suggest that there should be a member of the student counselling service within each institution with explicit responsibility for ensuring that the needs of the part-time students are addressed.

The rest of this chapter looks at some specific areas of student difficulties that have been identified above.

Difficulties arising from employment

The questionnaire asked those respondents in current employment for the number of hours they worked in a normal working week, 'including overtime and any other paid part-time work'. The mean (and median) response was 38 hours. Almost one quarter of those in paid employment normally worked for over forty hours per week or more (Table 6.8). For the remainder, the main difficulty associated with hours of employment seems to arise not from excessive hours of work in a 'normal' week but from the occurrence of abnormal weeks. In many types of employment, workloads are unevenly distributed and variation in the amplitude of cycles of work pressure (dealing with rush orders, urgent

Table 6.8   Number of hours worked per week by those in current employment.

Hours	%
Under 30	11
31–40	66
41–50	20
Over 50	3
Total	100

reports, computer crashes, etc.) causes problems for part-time undergraduates. A *majority* of the respondents in current employment claimed that they had had to miss some classes because of work commitments. When asked 'roughly what proportion of classes have you missed to date because of work commitments?', these students responded as shown in Table 6.9. It is reasonable to assume that the higher the proportion of missed classes, the more likely it is that the student will make a personal contribution to the non-completion statistics.

Problems associated with work pressures extend beyond the inability to attend classes. A total of 47 per cent of the respondents reported that they had experienced being unable to complete required reading or course work because of work requirements.

These findings appear to emphasize the need to achieve flexibility in structuring part-time degree courses. Arrangements that allow students to vary the load of their studies at different times in response to changes in work commitments would seem to be desirable.

Difficulties arising from domestic commitments

It was shown in Chapter 2 that the majority of the students are married. Of these, a majority have children and a spouse in full-time paid employment. It is inevitable that domestic pressures will sometimes become severe and impact on

Table 6.9   Percentage of classes missed due to work commitments.

% of classes missed	% of respondents
1–5%	66
More than 5% but less than 10%	22
Between 10% and 20%	9
More than 20%	4
Total	100

Table 6.10 Percentage of classes missed due to domestic commitments.

% of classes missed	% of respondents
1–5%	83
More than 5% but less than 10%	13
Between 10% and 20%	3
More than 20%	1
Total	100

the students' degree studies. For example, as shown above, almost 20 per cent of students had encountered increased study difficulties as a result of moving house. And, presumably, changes in domestic circumstances would have been a contributing factor in many cases to the decision to move house.

Over 30 per cent of the respondents reported that they had missed some classes because of domestic commitments. These students were then asked 'roughly what proportion of classes have you missed due to domestic commitments'. The results are shown in Table 6.10. In addition, 34 per cent answered 'yes' to the question 'Have you ever been unable to complete required reading or course work on time *because of domestic commitments?*'

Difficulties arising from travel to college

It is clear that part-time students' time is at a premium, with significant claims made upon it by attendance at classes, private study, work commitments and domestic commitments. To this list can be added travel time. Many of the respondents lived and/or worked a surprisingly long distance from their college (Table 6.11).

Table 6.11 Distance from home and work to college.

	% of respondents	
Miles	Distance from home to college	Distance from work to college
Less than 5	28	34
6–10	23	21
11–20	25	22
21–30	10	10
31–40	6	5
Over 40	8	8
Total	100	100

Table 6.12   Average number of journeys to college per week.

No.	%
1	37
2	54
3	6
more than 3	3
Total	100

The median distance between home and college was 10 miles, with a mean of 16 miles. Almost a quarter (24 per cent) live more than 20 miles from their college. The median distance between work and college was 10 miles, with a mean of 16 miles. A total of 23 per cent work more than 20 miles from college.

Most part-time undergraduates have to travel to college at least twice each week to attend their course. Therefore, with the sort of weekly mileage that many of the part-time students are clocking up, it is small wonder that a significant number would appreciate some element of distance learning integrated into their taught courses.

A key question, however, is how much time is taken up travelling to and from college to attend their courses (Table 6.13). Approximately half of the students spend more than 2 hours per week travelling to attend classes. They presumably spend yet more time travelling in any weeks that they make additional journeys to use other college facilities such as the library.

For over two-thirds of the respondents, their car was the most frequently used mode of transport and a further one-quarter normally used public transport. Those students that use public transport can use at least some of their time for reading. One wonders whether course providers could make greater use of cassette tapes as a means of tuition. The range of materials available on cassette tapes has substantially increased in recent years, and this is a resource that could be investigated. Alternatively, taped lectures would be an innovation for which many part-time students might be grateful (see Gibbs *et al.*, 1984).

Table 6.13   Average weekly travel time to/from college.

Hours	%
Less than 1	15
1–2	36
2–4	37
4–6	8
Over 6	4
Total	100

Financial difficulties

The financial cost of taking a part-time degree is clearly a factor in the decision to enrol and also a factor affecting non-completion. This study did not cover those who were deterred from enrolling by financial costs (the experience of the Open University would be relevant here), but it did explore the financial dimension of the experience of those who were enrolled.

About 60 per cent of the respondents reported that they received some financial support with their part-time studies. For those who were in current paid employment, this proportion was much higher (see below), as employers were the main source of financial assistance. A total of 95 per cent of the respondents who were in current paid employment reported that their employers (or supervisors) were aware that they were taking their CNAA part-time degree course. Of these, the large majority received some form of financial support (Table 6.14). It can be seen that 80 per cent of the respondents in current paid employment received at least partial assistance with their fees from their employers.

In general, Table 6.14 gives an impression of a supportive attitude by employers. This raises the question of whether course leaders could facilitate the manifestation of this goodwill by providing students with estimates of some of the cost elements (e.g. estimated cost of book and equipment requirements) and by certifying the reasonableness of items such as travel costs to and from college. This would presumably make it easier for students to claim support and it would probably make it easier also for employers to provide the support.

Only 16 per cent of the respondents had sought assistance from local (or central) government and it is notable that of those a majority had been unsuccessful. The issue of assistance from public funds for part-time degree course students is, of course, a vexed one (see Bourner, 1979). Presumably, the proportion that did not seek such assistance reflects an assessment of the likelihood of success. This is illustrated by the rather sad comment made by one

Table 6.14 Types of employer support for those students in current paid employment.

	%
Employer pays or refunds the whole of the fees	65
Time off to attend classes with pay	51
Travelling allowance	38
Additional study leave (e.g. before exams)	36
Use of employer's facilities (e.g. laboratory, library, computer)	34
Book and/or equipment allowance	26
Pays or refunds *part* of fees	15
Time off to attend classes without pay	6
Reduced workload	4

Table 6.15   Proportion of average annual cost of pursuing course accounted for by various items.

Items	%
Course fees (tuition and registration)	42
Extra travel costs resulting from taking the course	29
Books	14
Extra expenditure on food eaten outside home resulting from taking the course	9
Other equipment, stationery, materials	6
Total	100

of the respondents who was told that a grant 'would be decided on merit and decided not to pursue the matter'.

Less than 1 per cent of the respondents had obtained help from a professional body or trade union. Other sources of financial assistance mentioned by respondents included relatives and private educational trust funds.

The respondents were asked for the 'approximate *annual* cost' of taking their courses 'whether borne by yourself or from some other source'. Table 6.15 includes those items that were identified by all or most of the respondents and shows the mean values. For most of the respondents, course fees represent a minority component of the total financial cost of taking their course. It is also worth noting that travel costs are the second largest cost item, accounting for, on average, more than twice the costs of books.

Other items of cost of undertaking part-time degree level studies mentioned by the respondents included:

- Loss of earnings (including loss of overtime earnings),
- stopped or reduced part-time work,
- lost promotion opportunities,
- child-care and babysitting costs,
- typing of projects/assignments,
- residential weekends,
- car parking,
- second car for spouse,
- extra convenience foods,
- school dinners for children, and
- bought clothes instead of handmade.

The last question on the questionnaire concerning potential financial problems asked 'Considering *all* the costs involved, has taking this course caused financial difficulty for you or your family?', and then presented the possible range of responses shown in Table 6.16. Almost 80 per cent of the students were not experiencing difficulties with the financial costs of their courses. The corollary, of course, is that over 20 per cent were experiencing some difficulty. It is interesting in this context to note that the fees for part-time degree courses in the polytechnics and colleges of higher education are, for the most part,

Table 6.16 Financial impact of taking course.

Assessment	%
Can meet the costs fairly easily	43
No problem at all	36
Quite difficult to meet the costs	21
Severe hardship	1
Total	100

significantly less than university part-time degree courses, whether these be at the Open University or conventional universities (see Wagner and Watts, 1976).

It is important to remember the remarks that opened this section. This study looked at the financial impact on those who enrolled on part-time degree courses. It did not address the issue of those who were deterred from enrolling by the financial cost. Presumably, all the respondents believed that they could cope with the financial costs at the time that they started their courses. And it should be remembered that over 15 per cent of the respondents found coping with the financial costs more difficult than they had expected.

Summary

1. *Overall assessment.* For over 90 per cent of the respondents, their CNAA part-time degree courses were rated as 'roughly as expected' or 'better than expected'. A similar percentage would have recommended their course to a friend in a similar position to themselves when they started. Existing students are potentially powerful agents for the recruitment of new students. Very high levels of satisfaction were expressed with the relationships between staff and students, course content and the helpfulness of the staff. In general, the students expressed a higher level of overall satisfaction with the courses than with the college facilities.

2. *Specific strengths and weaknesses.* The elements of the courses that provided least satisfaction were the arrangements for students to make their voices heard in course evaluation, feedback to students on their performance and progress and opportunities to vary the pace of their studies. The respondents expressed high levels of satisfaction with library opening hours and library loan regulations, but less satisfaction with the *availability* of books and journals recommended by staff. The two factors that produced the highest proportions of dissatisfied respondents were refectory/canteen facilities and pre-school child-care facilities. Interpretation of the latter factor is difficult, however, as it was inapplicable to a relatively large proportion of the respondents.

3. *Perceived standards.* Three-quarters of the respondents thought that CNAA part-time degree courses are of equivalent standard to CNAA full-time degree

courses. Of the remainder, a majority thought that the part-time degree courses were of a higher standard. However, they felt less confident about the perceptions of others. They thought that their employers were less inclined to rate the relative standard of their CNAA part-time degree courses as highly as they did themselves and they were even less optimistic about the perceptions of academics in institutions of higher education. This is significant in the light of the findings that a substantial proportion of the students planned to engage in further study after their undergraduate programmes.

4. *Student difficulties.* For about three-quarters of the students, the difficulties, overall, had been roughly as expected when they enrolled. Of the remainder, over three times as many had experienced greater difficulties than expected than had experienced less difficulties than expected.

A majority of the respondents had experienced more difficulty in finding the time to study than they had expected. Most of these perceived this as a problem of time management ('organizing my time in an efficient way').

Coping with the stress of examinations and developing appropriate study skills was more difficult than expected for more than 20 per cent of the respondents. A substantial proportion of the respondents reported that coping with the competing demands of family, job and 'other interests' had proved more difficult than expected. Almost 40 per cent said that a change in their job responsibilities had increased their difficulties and for almost 20 per cent changes in family responsibilities accounted for increased difficulties. Moving house was also identified as a factor that increased the difficulties of a substantial proportion of the students (18 per cent).

A majority of the respondents had had to miss classes because of work commitments and almost half reported that they had been unable to complete required reading or coursework because of work requirements. Over 30 per cent of the respondents had missed some classes because of domestic commitments and about a third reported that they had been unable to complete required reading or coursework because of domestic commitments.

5. *Travel.* Approximately half of the respondents spent more than 2 hours per week travelling to attend classes – this does not include any additional journeys to make use of other college facilities such as the library. The median distance from home to college was 10 miles (the mean was 16 miles). Almost a quarter live more than 20 miles from the college.

6. *Finances.* About 60 per cent of the students who completed the questionnaire said that they had received some form of financial support for their part-time studies. Most of this support came from employers. Most of the minority who had sought assistance from local (or central) government had been unsuccessful. Only 20 per cent reported that they were experiencing difficulty with the financial costs of their course. However, as is shown in Chapter 8, for those that do experience such difficulty this can be an important element in the likelihood of not completing their course.

7 | Course Development Issues

Other chapters in the book have looked at specific areas of relevance to the development of new and existing courses. The project also explored some issues pertaining to course development not easily located within the subject matter of those chapters. These areas are addressed here.

Intermediate awards

Some courses provide students with certification for successful completion of an intermediate stage of their degree course. This is believed to be more common on part-time courses than on full-time courses. A total of 14 per cent of the survey respondents said that their courses provided for such intermediate awards. Of these, the majority were eligible for a diploma award and most of the remainder were eligible for a certificate award. Some students reported that they could complete with a non-honours degree if they decided not to proceed to the full requirements of an honours degree.

The respondents that were eligible for an intermediate award were asked how important they regarded this facility. Eighty per cent said that they attached at least some importance to it. Over a third saw it as 'very important' Table 7.1).

It is possible that students for whom an intermediate qualification was important would have sought out a course with this facility. Those who were on

Table 7.1 Importance of intermediate awards to eligible students.

Assessment	%
Very important	37
Quite important	43
Unimportant	20
Total	100

Table 7.2   Impact of intermediate awards on the attractiveness of courses: Views of the ineligible students.

Assessment	%
Much more attractive	37
A little more attractive	31
Would make no difference	31
Total	100

courses that did not confer eligibility for an intermediate award were asked for their opinion on whether or not the introduction of such an award would make their course more attractive. The results show that these students too were favourably disposed towards intermediate certification (Table 7.2). Over two-thirds of these respondents thought that it would make a positive impact on the attractiveness of their course. Over one-third thought that it would make their course 'much more attractive'.

Considerable difficulties confront the student in sustaining high level study over the necessarily long duration of a part-time degree course. Domestic and professional circumstances can change in unpredictable ways, so that the probability of successful completion cannot be so high as for full-time students. For this reason it is desirable that part-time students perceive objectives that are realistically attainable in their not too distant futures. Moreover, it is also desirable to make provisions that allow for the students to adjust their objectives as the course progresses.

Some potential students are unsure of their capacity to complete a full degree course. Such students are likely to draw confidence from the presence of an intermediate award for the successful completion of the initial stages of the degree course.

In the light of the student responses reported in this section, and as the introduction of such intermediate certification is a relatively straightforward business, it is suggested that its merits should be examined by courses that have not done so. It is possible that it could have a favourable impact on course recruitment.

Residentials

The questionnaire asked 'Does your course involve any period(s) of residential or "block" attendance (e.g. weekend school)' Approximately one-third of the respondents answered 'yes'.

Opinions differ on the merits of 'residentials' on part-time degree courses. On the one hand, it raises the cost of part-time study to the students and is resource-intensive for staff. These are important considerations as part-time degree courses are not well-resourced. On the other hand, residentials provide an opportunity to make available to part-time students a wider range of study methods and learning activities, and they help to develop social cohesiveness among students. The latter can be especially valuable in developing students' appreciation of each other as a learning resource. In the light of the findings of this project, a residential orientated towards enhancing study skills, improved time management and the development of self-help groups would seem to be worth considering as a way of starting most part-time degree courses.

Full-time study

It may be that the dichotomy between full-time and part-time study has been too tightly drawn and that some thought should be given to facilitating greater permeability between study modes. It is conceivable that some part-time degree course students, while unable to undertake a full-time course (due, for example, to financial commitments), would be able to undertake some *part* of their degree course on a full-time basis.

The questionnaire asked 'If it were possible to spend a period during your present course on full-time study (with a mature student's grant) would you be interested in doing this?' This was clearly a very speculative question and it was understood at the time that the questionnaire was designed so that the interpretation of the phrase 'if it were possible' was left unresolved for the student. Notwithstanding this, it did seem worth exploring, if only tentatively, attitudes to this suggestion. The responses are shown in Table 7.3.

This question was followed in the questionnaire by a much more specific enquiry into student attitudes to the possibility of commuting the final 2 years of part-time study by 1 year of full-time study (on the assumption that a mature student's grant would be available). Interest in this question stemmed from two sources. First, this option is actually available on some part-time degree courses. Secondly, where it is available, there are various factors that make this option less of a financial burden than many students (or staff) appear to believe. In particular, the academic year straddles two tax years so that tax relief from the preceding and succeeding years can be claimed, a mature student's grant is usually larger than is often appreciated and the academic 'year' is, in fact, only

Table 7.3 Interest in full-time study for part of the course.

Assessment	%
Definitely	32
Probably	15
Possibly	18
Probably not	19
Definitely not	16
Total	100

Table 7.4   Interest in completing final stage of part-time course by full-time study.

Assessment	%
Definitely	34
Probably	16
Possibly	17
Probably not	18
Definitely not	15
Total	100

about 8 months (see Bourner, 1979). The findings from the survey's respondents are shown in Table 7.4.

It is interesting that, compared with the previous question, this more specific suggestion produced a slightly more positive response. Over one-third of the respondents said 'definitely' and over two-thirds expressed some level of positive interest. The main problem with this proposal is, however, an anomaly within the student grant regulations whereby a student who undertakes part of a part-time degree at his/her own expense becomes, thereby, ineligible for a mandatory award for completing the final stage by full-time study. However, such a student who *transfers* to the final year of another course *is* eligible for a mandatory award.

There are two clear policy implications that follow from these results:

1. Because, at most institutions, part-time degree courses exist alongside corresponding full-time degree courses, arrangements could be made to facilitate transfers into the final year of the latter from the former. This may require better communication between the two modes than exists in some colleges. And, of course, students would need to be made aware of these arrangements.
2. The anomaly in the student grants regulations mentioned above should be removed.

Mixed mode classes

At some colleges, part-time and full-time courses in the same subject maintain a clear distance, being separately administered and, for the most part, taught by separate groups of staff. There is some evidence that resource constraints are bringing the courses together (see Bourner and McQueen, 1983). Classes at which part-time and full-time students are taught together are comparatively rare. Some would applaud this as enabling the particular needs of each group of students to be addressed. Others would argue that in mixed mode classes, the educational experience is enhanced by the contribution of each group to the other.

Overall, 23 per cent of the respondents had attended classes on their course at which full-time students were also present. The incidence of mixed mode classes appears to increase through the first to the last year of the course. This may reflect a view that the particular needs of the two groups are most dissimilar when the students are at an early stage of their studies, or it may simply reflect the fact that it is required to produce student groups with viable numbers to sustain an attractive range of subject options at the final stages of the degree courses (combined presumably with the impact of non-completion on student numbers over the degree course).

A significant factor in whether part-time and full-time students are joined for some classes is whether the students think that it would or would not enhance their learning experience. The questionnaire provides some evidence on this matter as far as part-time students are concerned (Table 7.5).

If full-time students joined part-time students for some classes, over 20 per cent of the respondents would welcome it compared with only 5 per cent who would object strongly. A total of 60 per cent were amenable to the suggestion compared to 30 per cent who found the suggestion unattractive. On balance, then, there is some net support for the idea among part-time students. Whether full-time students would favour the idea (especially if it involved some evening attendance) is more problematic.

Weekend attendance

In view of the declining unit of real resource per student over the last decade, it is important to be aware of the value that students place on various college facilities. It may be felt that decisions on the availability of college facilities are insufficiently informed by the views of part-time students if only because their limited time at college gives them less time to promote their views (e.g. through the medium of the students' union).

Some evidence on this issue is provided by answers to the question: 'If you

Table 7.5 Part-time students' attitudes to classes including full-time students.

Assessment	%
I would object strongly	5
I prefer classes with other part-time students only	25
Indifferent/don't know	11
I wouldn't mind	39
I would welcome some classes with full-time students	21
Total	101

Table 7.6   Value placed on extending evening or weekend facilities.

Assessment	%
Weekends	32
Evenings	22
Equal value	23
Neither would be of much value to me	23
Total	100

were given a choice between further availability of college facilities (library, computer, study rooms, etc.) in the evenings *or* at weekends, which would be of greater value to you?' Neither of these suggestions secured a majority among the respondents, but more favoured extended availability at weekends than in the evenings (Table 7.6).

There is, of course, a large difference between questions of *extending* the availability of facilities and questions of *reducing* the availability of facilities. However, an enquiry into the latter might have been interpreted by the students as providing information which could have been used by some colleges as a mandate for further cuts in facilities in the event of a continued fall in the unit of real resource.

There was little support for the suggestion that a session of evening attendance be replaced by an equivalent period of attendance on Saturday mornings, despite the fact that a few part-time courses do currently include attendance on Saturday mornings (Table 7.7). Over half of the respondents emphatically opposed this suggestion and three-quarters gave some form of negative response. Of course, these students were recruited to courses with the existing pattern of attendance, and students recruited to courses with Saturday classes might have responded differently but the results will, no doubt, be greeted with relief by many college staff.

Table 7.7   Interest in substituting Saturday morning for evening attendance.

Assessment	%
Definitely not	54
Probably not	21
Possibly	10
Probably	7
Definitely	8
Total	100

Summary

1. *Intermediate awards*. A total of 14 per cent of the respondents said that their courses provided for some form of intermediate award. Of these, 80 per cent said that they attached at least some importance to it and over a third saw it as 'very important'. Of the respondents on courses that did not provide for intermediate awards, most (68 per cent) thought the introduction of such an award would have a positive impact on the attractiveness of their course and over a third thought that it would make their course 'much more attractive'.

2. *Patterns of attendance*. Approximately one-third of the respondents reported that their course involved some form of 'block attendance' such as a weekend school. About two-thirds of the students expressed some level of positive interest in the possibility of completing the final stage of their degree course by full-time study. About one-third expressed a high level of positive interest. Steps to facilitate this possibility should be encouraged.

3. *Classes with full-time students*. Overall, 23 per cent of the respondents had attended classes on their courses at which full-time students were also present. The incidence of mixed mode classes appears to rise from the first to the last years of the courses.

On balance, there was support among the respondents for the suggestion that full-time students join part-time students for some classes. Sixty per cent were amenable to the suggestion compared to 30 per cent who found the idea unattractive. As for the stronger feelings, over 20 per cent said that they would welcome it compared with only 5 per cent who would object strongly.

8 | Non-completion

Little is known about student non-completion on part-time courses. Even less is known about student non-completion on part-time first degree courses where the issue is of particular importance. It might reasonably be expected that non-completion rates are high on these advanced courses, which are often of 5 years' duration. Non-completion can involve a loss to the student in terms of time, money and self-esteem, and possibly also a rejection of further formal education. From the perspective of the educational system as a whole, it can involve a waste of resources. From the perspective of the course and institution, it is also clearly a problem. High rates of non-completion are often taken as an indication of poor course and/or college performance. Also, heavy student wastage can result in very small numbers in the more advanced stages of part-time degree courses with adverse educational consequences for the students that remain (including constraining the range of advanced stage options that are available to the students). In addition, low student retention can act as a disincentive to the provision of part-time degree courses in the context of the relatively meagre resourcing of part-time courses.

The objectives of this chapter are to:

1. Identify the extent of student non-completion among part-time students on CNAA first degree courses.
2. Compare the Open University experience of non-completion with that of CNAA part-time degree courses.
3. Identify *student* and *course* characteristics that are systematically related to student non-completion.

Most of the information for this chapter was collected by means of a short follow-up questionnaire sent to the students one year after the first questionnaire. The follow-up enquiry asked them to indicate whether:

1. They were still enrolled on the course.
2. They had completed the course.
3. They had withdrawn from the course with an intermediate award.
4. They had withdrawn from the course without any intermediate award.
5. They had failed the course.
6. They did not fall into any of the above categories.

The responses were to be linked to the datafiles containing the results of the first questionnaire, so that student retention could be cross-tabulated against the information already held to identify factors associated with non-completion.

After two reminder letters, approximately 2300 respondents had supplied the required information (80 per cent response rate), leaving a little under 600 non-responders. The non-completion rates seemed low for those that had responded to the follow up enquiry (less than 10 per cent). There was a strong feeling among the project officers that the 'non-completers' were disproportionately represented among the 20 per cent who had not responded. Moreover, we felt that this problem would seriously affect the validity and usefulness of the exercise.

We decided to telephone the non-respondents about their subsequent progress on their course, but this strategy did not prove successful as it was very time-consuming and the 'strike rate' was low. Finally, we adopted an alternative approach which involved contacting the course leaders. This proved to be very successful and confirmed our suspicion of response bias in the returns to the student follow-up questionnaire. The information supplied by the course leaders on 20 per cent of the students accounted for 45 per cent of the non-completers. Eventually, we obtained information on the subsequent progress of the entire 100 per cent of the 2876 students who had completed the original questionnaire.

Non-completion and student wastage

Non-completion is sometimes regarded as a (negative) indicator of course and college performance. The rationale for this is presumably that the more successful that courses and colleges are in meeting the needs of the students, the less inclined they are to leave. On the other hand, there are those who would contend that most of the drop-out by part-time students is due to factors outside the control of the courses or the colleges. A study by Woodley and McIntosh (1980) asked Open University students who had not completed final registration to give the main reason why, and 77 per cent were related to domestic and work circumstances. Another study at the Open University (drop-out rates from third-level mathematics courses) gave a questionnaire with 12 possible reasons for drop-out. A total of 61 per cent of the respondents gave domestic and job factors as the main reason (Phythian and Clements, 1982). In view of this, it might be concluded that there is little that courses and colleges can do to reduce student drop-out. Woodley and Parlett (1983), however, reject this argument on three grounds:

1. The response rates for drop-out questionnaires are usually low (51 and 33 per cent respectively, for the studies mentioned in the previous paragraph) leaving considerable scope for response bias.
2. The reasons given are likely to be rationalizations. Students who find the academic level of a course too demanding are likely to explain away their

inability to cope in terms of domestic pressures such as domestic or work commitments.

3. The decision to withdraw is usually the result of a combination of factors not a single reason. Woodley and Parlett (1983) suggest that a typical expanded reason would be: 'Work pressures meant that I had less time for O.U. study – but I guess that I would have stuck with the course if I had found it more interesting.'

The last point is particularly telling. It implies that the more successful a course is in meeting the needs of a student, the more severe must be the domestic and work pressures to cause the student to withdraw.

This issue, however, is complicated by the fact that there can be some very positive reasons for the non-completion of a part-time degree course. These include:

1. The student who is sufficiently enthused by his/her part-time degree course studies to make whatever personal (domestic/employment) sacrifices are necessary to transfer to a full-time course. This is not a fanciful example, as many part-time courses are designed to run alongside a corresponding full-time course facilitating transfer between the two as the student's circumstances change.

2. The student whose part-time degree studies contribute to promotion at work, which brings with it additional responsibilities that leave insufficient time for part-time degree level studies. This, too, is not a fanciful example in the light of the findings reported in Chapter 4 of the heavy emphasis placed on enhancement of career prospects as a reason for part-time degree studies and the finding that for a substantial proportion (40 per cent), changes in job responsibilities had increased the difficulty of pursuing the course.

In these cases, it may be appropriate to treat non-completion as a *positive* indicator of course success. There is a further more potent reason for reluctance to use non-completion rates as an indicator of (negative) course performance and this derives from its behavioural consequences. This can be most easily appreciated by analogy with labour turnover in the employment relationship. The literature on labour turnover within organizations identifies two basic types of personnel policies to reduce labour turnover: retention policies and selection policies. An organization can take steps that will retain existing job encumbents and it can recruit job applicants with characteristics associated with long expected duration of employment. The position of part-time degree courses is similar. Colleges and courses can adopt policies and practices to retain the part-time students that enrol and they can select for student retention.

While the former is normally commendable, it certainly is not if students are discouraged from transferring to other courses that might better meet their needs. Again one can look to analogies with the 'locking-in' devices that some organizations employ to retain employees. Passive discouragement could also take the form of a reluctance to develop intermediate awards, as a result of anxiety regarding so many students taking the intermediate award option that the viability of the final stage of the degree would be threatened.

The latter type of policy (selection for retention) is commendable when it takes such forms as counselling applicants to ensure that the course really meets their needs. However, it can also lead to an excessively 'safe' entry policy. For example, it is shown later in this chapter that non-completion rates are higher for those in manual employment and those with lower incomes. It would be difficult to support an entry policy that discriminates against these groups. The use of non-completion rates as a performance indicator can imply tacit or unwitting support for illiberal and restrictive entry policies.

There is a further reason for concern with non-completion and that is its impact on the educational experience of those who remain. High rates of non-completion can result in low student numbers being retained for the advanced stages of part-time degree courses. Small numbers may mean more individual attention but many educational methods (particularly those involving group work) lose their potency when the number of students becomes very small. A seminar comprising two or three students can be much less rich as an educational experience than one with twice that number. Also, if this situation leads to the contraction or limitation of the range of final-year options, it can hardly be regarded as being in the students' educational interests. It means that a smaller percentage of the students at the advanced stage will have available to them the subjects that best meet their educational needs.

The conclusion of this discussion is that non-completion is very important, but as a general performance indicator it is a blunt instrument that is likely to encourage some undesirable practices.

Part-time courses are not well-resourced and high rates of non-completion usually raise difficulties for those administering part-time degree courses (particularly at the advanced stages) and this itself is a discipline. The evidence from the course leaders' questionnaire showed a high level of awareness of the problem of non-completion. Part-time courses with high rates of non-completion probably need help rather than censure. It would be of assistance to those responsible for running part-time degree courses, in terms of both prediction and control, if factors that are associated with student retention could be identified, and that is the main objective of the rest of this chapter.

The pattern of non-completion

The subsequent progress of the 2876 respondents to the students' questionnaire is shown in Table 8.1 by their status one year after the original questionnaire. Almost two-thirds of the students were still enrolled on their course, over 20 per cent had successfully completed their course, and 11 per cent had withdrawn without any form of award. Only 3 per cent had failed and only 1 per cent had left with an intermediate award. The small size of the last percentage is worth noting. It compares with the finding that 14 per cent of the respondents were on courses that provided for some form of intermediate award and that this form of

Table 8.1   Status of the respondents one year after initial contact.

Response	No.	%
Still enrolled on the course	1843	64
Successfully completed the course	598	21
Withdrawn from the course without an intermediate award	311	11
Failed	75	3
Withdrawn from the course with an intermediate award	29	1
None of the above	20	1
Total	2876	100

reassurance was valued by these respondents. Any suspicion that intermediate awards might result in mass desertion of the courses at the intermediate stage is without foundation.

Table 8.1 gives an overall idea of the order of magnitudes of the various categories of subsequent progress of the students. However, those who have been involved in administering a part-time degree course will be aware that the rate of non-completion is highest in the year that students join a course. It is clear from Table 8.2 that the probability that a student will successfully progress to the next year of a course rises with the number of years that a student has been enrolled on a course. In particular, the more years that students have been enrolled the smaller is the proportion who withdraw without any form of award.

The reasons for this phenomenon are probably several. Many new students, no doubt, experience an 'induction crisis' during the early period of their enrolment. Academically weaker students are likely to discover at a fairly early stage that they have underestimated the demands of the course. Where there is a mismatch between the course and a student's needs, this is likely to become

Table 8.2   Status of respondents (percentages) by student year of course.

Response	Year			
	1	*2*	*3*	*4+*
Still enrolled or successfully completed	74	87	94	95
Withdrawn from the course without intermediate award	19	9	5	2
Failed	5	2	1	1
Withdrawn from the course with an intermediate award	1	2	1	1
None of the above	1	1	0[a]	1
Total				
%	100	101	101	100
No.	1033	762	645	436

[a] Less than 0.5 per cent.

apparent quite soon after enrolment. Last, but not least, the longer that a student has been enrolled, the greater is his/her investment in the course and the greater will be the incentive to protect that investment by continued enrolment.

In interpreting Table 8.2, it should be clear that it refers to the number of years (including current year) that *respondents* had been enrolled on their courses. Transfers from another course will appear as 'new' students even though they enter on the second, third, fourth or even fifth year of their new course. Also, it should be appreciated that not all courses are of the same length. In particular, some are intended to 'top up' other courses of higher education. Such courses will have students graduating in 2–3 years of enrolment.

In Tables 8.3 and 8.4, this issue is addressed by identifying separately the results for respondents on courses of 3 years or less in duration from those on courses that normally last 4 years or more. In both tables, the proportion of students who successfully progressed to the next year of the course is an increasing function of the number of years of the course that they completed. Also, the proportion of students who withdrew with no form of award fell with the number of years completed.

If the data in Tables 8.3 and 8.4 represent a steady-state situation, then it might be inferred that the cumulative cohort rate of non-completion for a 3-year part-time degree course is about 15 per cent and for a 5-year part-time degree about 50 per cent. These, however, are underestimates, because of the way that the data were collected. The original questionnaire was distributed in December/January (about 4 months after the start of the academic year) and a considerable amount of the first-year student drop-out will have occurred by then, so that the true figure for non-completion in the first year is likely to be significantly higher. It can be concluded, therefore, that the average cumulative

Table 8.3 Status of respondents (percentages) by student year of course: Courses lasting 3 years or less.

Response	Year		
	1	*2*	*3 or more*[a]
Still enrolled or successfully completed	91	97	99
Withdrawn from the course without intermediate award	5	2	1
Failed	1	0[b]	0[b]
Withdrawn from the course with an intermediate award	1	0	0
None of the above	1	0	0
Total			
%	99	99	100
No.	131	147	153

[a] Includes those who had retaken a year of the course.
[b] Less than 0.5 per cent.

Table 8.4   Status of respondents (percentages) by student year of course: Courses lasting 4 years or more.

	Year			
Response	*1*	*2*	*3*	*4 or more[a]*
Still enrolled or successfully completed	71	84	92	94
Withdrawn from the course without intermediate award	21	11	6	2
Failed	6	2	1	1
Withdrawn from the course with an intermediate award	1	2	1	1
None of the above	1	1	0[b]	1
Total				
%	100	100	100	99
No.	902	615	497	431

[a] Includes those who had retaken a year of the course.
[b] Less than 0.5 per cent.

cohort rate of non-completion for a 3-year part-time degree course is *at least* 15 per cent and for a 5-year part-time degree course *at least* 50 per cent.

The major difference between Tables 8.3 and 8.4 is that the level of non-completion among the first-year students is much higher for the longer courses. The proportion of first-year students who either failed or withdrew without any form of award is 27 per cent for the longer courses compared with only 6 per cent for the shorter courses. There are many possible reasons for this. Students enrolled on the shorter courses normally have previous experience of higher education and are therefore more aware of the level of academic difficulty, they tend to be better qualified, are less likely to be on evening-only courses, are more likely to have employer support, are more likely to have previous experience of study at the same college, and are more likely to have successfully completed a previous course of part-time study.

Later in this chapter it will be shown that these are all factors associated with successful completion of a part-time degree course. There is another factor that is relevant: they have fewer years of further study to complete, so that the prospect of successful completion is that much more imminent.

It is quite possible that the expected number of years remaining to completion exerts an influence that is independent of the number of years completed. Table 8.5 explores this possibility. The information in Table 8.5 confirms the suggestion that the expected number of years to completion has an effect on non-completion rates that is additional to the number of years completed.

Hopefully, the magnitude and structure of wastage revealed in Tables 8.1–8.5 will be helpful to those engaged in course development. In particular, it should be helpful to those developing new part-time degree courses in predicting the likely levels of student retention of the final stages of the courses. In the case of new course development, however, there is a further factor to take into account, which is explored in the next section.

Table 8.5 Status of respondents (percentages) by expected years to completion.

	Expected years to completion				
Response	*5 or more*	*4*	*3*	*2*	*1 or less*
Still enrolled or successfully completed	70	74	86	95	96
Withdrawn from the course without intermediate award	23	19	10	4	2
Failed	6	5	2	0[a]	1
Withdrawn from the course with an intermediate award	0[a]	1	1	2	1
None of the above	1	1	0[a]	0[a]	1
Total					
%	100	100	99	101	101
No.	351	436	645	762	1033

[a]Less than 0.5 per cent.

New courses

In the sample of 66 courses involved in this study, 16 were 'immature' in the sense that they had been developed sufficiently recently that no students had yet graduated. Some of these 'new' courses had, as yet, only first- or second-year students enrolled. Table 8.6 compares the experience of non-completion on these courses with the other 'mature' courses.

Comparing the last two columns of Table 8.6 it is clear that the second year retention rate is lower for the new courses and that this is largely accounted for by the higher proportion of students who withdrew without any form of award. The same conclusion holds also for the first-year students, though the differences here are less marked.

The conclusion that can be drawn from Table 8.6 is that the problem of non-completion is likely to be particularly severe during the early life of a course until course teams develop experience. It is at this stage that there is greatest need for support and assistance for course teams in dealing with the problem of non-completion.

Distribution of non-completion across subject groups

In the light of the findings in the previous sections, it makes little sense to simply compare the non-completion rates across subject groups without regard to the distribution of students across the years of the courses. For this reason, and

Table 8.6　Progress of respondents by maturity of course.

Response	Year 1		Year 2	
	New (%)	Mature (%)	New (%)	Mature (%)
Still enrolled[a]	72	74	79	88
Withdrawn from the course without intermediate award	23	18	17	8
Failed	4	6	2	2
Withdrawn from the course with an intermediate award	1	1	3	1
None of the above	0[b]	1	0	1
Total				
%	100	100	101	100
No.	190	843	107	655

[a] Or successfully completed.
[b] Less than 0.5 per cent.

because the first-year students are the group who are most at risk, Table 8.7 compares the progress of those respondents who, at the time of the initial questionnaire, had been enrolled for one year or less.

The first-year retention rate is highest for education and lowest for the social sciences. In the light of the earlier analysis, it may come as no surprise to discover that the subject group with the highest proportion of 'short' courses (normal duration of 3 years or less) is education. Science is the subject group with the next highest proportion of 'short' courses. There are no such 'short' courses among the social science courses included in the survey.

For the most part, the proportion of students who withdrew without any form of award mirrors the pattern of the first-year retention percentages shown in the top of Table 8.7. The one reservation to this statement can be found in the figures for student failure. These are more erratically distributed across the subject groups. Thus comparing business studies with engineering/technology, which have the same retention rate, the former has a much higher wastage rate but the latter has a much higher failure rate. Again, comparing art/humanities with social sciences, the former has a higher wastage rate but the latter has a much higher failure rate.

The main conclusion that emerges from Table 8.7, however, is that it is difficult to discern a pure subject effect on non-completion that is independent of incidence of 'short' courses among the subject groups.

Comparisons with Open University non-completion

The source of most of the information on non-completion of Open University undergraduate courses in this chapter is Woodley and Parlett (1983). They used

Table 8.7 Progress of first-year students by subject group.

	Education (%)	Science (%)	Engineering/technology (%)	Business Studies (%)	Arts/humanities (%)	Social sciences (%)
Still enrolled[a]	93	79	75	75	64	59
Withdrawn from course without intermediate award	6	15	14	23	32	29
Failed	0	4	8	3	1	11
Withdrawn from course with intermediate award	0	1	1	0[b]	2	1
None of the above	0	1	2	0	0	1
Total						
%	99	100	100	101	99	101
No.	116	220	198	209	90	200

[a] Or successfully completed.
[b] Less than 0.5 per cent.

Table 8.8   Open University undergraduate progress in 1982.

	New students (%)	Continuing students (%)	Total (%)
Non-completion of final registration (base = all provisionally registered)	28	N/A	N/A
Withdrawal rate (base = all who finally registered)	17	27	24
Failure rate (base = all who sat exam)	6	7	6
Overall wastage rate (base = all who finally registered)	22	32	32

Source: Woodley and Parlett (1983).

data on Open University undergraduates in 1981 and 1982 (see Table 8.8; see also Woodley, 1987).

In the first year of study with the Open University, students register in the previous year, the courses start in February and they are finally registered in April. Finally, registered new students are those who have paid either the whole or the first instalment of their registration fee by the required date in April.

Woodley and Parlett (1983, p. 3) summarize the main points as:

- Nearly three out of ten new students did not complete final registration.
- One in four of the finally registered students did not sit any final exam.
- One in seventeen of those who sat a final exam did not gain any credit.
- Three out of ten finally registered students gained no course credit.

In the survey of undergraduates of CNAA part-time degree courses, the students would normally have started their courses in September, but our computed non-completion rates are based on those who were still on their courses by January. It is therefore most sensible to compare non-completion rates of CNAA part-time undergraduates with the non-completion rates of Open University undergraduates who were finally registered. More specifically, it seems reasonable to compare the Open University withdrawal rate for new students with the proportions of CNAA part-time undergraduates who withdrew with no form of award and who failed (see Table 8.9).

According to these results, student non-completion is higher in the first year on CNAA part-time undergraduates but for subsequent years the rate of non-completion is higher for Open University students. It seems that those who enrol on CNAA part-time degree courses experience the difficulties of adjustment (induction crisis) when they first enrol on their course, and that this is more severe (or they are less well-prepared for it) than that experienced by new Open University undergraduates. However, it also seems that this adjustment occurs only at the start of the CNAA part-time courses, whereas it recurs for the Open University students with each additional course that they take.

Table 8.9   Non-completion: Open University and CNAA part-time undergraduates.

	Withdrawal rate[a] (%)	Failure rate (%)	Overall wastage rate[a] (%)
New undergraduates			
Open University[b]	17	6	22
CNAA part-time[c]	20	5	25
Continuing students			
Open University	27	7	32
CNAA part-time[d]	7	1	8

Source: Woodley and Parlett (1983) and CNAA part-time undergraduate survey.
[a] Excludes students who left after successfully completing the requirements of an intermediate award.
[b] Base = all new students finally registered April 1982.
[c] Base = new students still registered at January 1985.
[d] Students enrolled on their second or subsequent years.

Subject groups

There is a marked contrast in wastage rates across subject groups. In the Open University, the wastage rates for mathematics and technology courses were above average, whereas the wastage rates for the arts and social sciences were below average. Precisely the reverse is the case for CNAA courses. Variation in the incidence of CNAA 'short' courses designed to 'top up' previous courses of higher education is probably the main explanation for this.

Sex

The experience of the Open University is that men are more likely than women to drop-out. On the CNAA part-time degree courses, there was no significant difference in the non-completion rates of men and women.

Age

Among new undergraduates with the Open University, the very young and the very old were more likely to drop out. For continuing students, the very young were more likely to drop out but the evidence for the very old was more mixed. For the CNAA students, it is difficult to discern any systematic variation in non-completion rates by age.

Previous educational qualifications

Referring to the Open University, Woodley and Parlett (1983, p. 9) conclude that, 'generally speaking, the lower a person's previous educational qualifications the more likely he or she was to drop out'. For the CNAA part-time degree courses, the matter is a little more complicated. Among the students who failed to progress, there was a higher proportion with qualifications of GCE 'A' level standard or below but there was also a higher proportion who already had degree level qualifications. Among the non-completers, there was a lower proportion with HNCs and with teaching certificates or diplomas.

Occupation

For undergraduates of the Open University, there were especially high wastage rates among those in manual occupations, the retired and unemployed and those in institutions (such as prisons and hospitals). Clearly, the last category does not apply to those taking CNAA part-time degree courses, but otherwise the same conclusion holds.

Accumulated credit

In general, the more Open University credits already held, the greater the likelihood of gaining some further Open University course credit during the year. The corresponding finding for the CNAA part-time degree students is that the more years that students have completed the lower the likelihood of dropping out.

Block release/residentials

In general, Open University courses with summer school had lower wastage rates than those without. For the CNAA part-time degree students, a related finding is that those who had attended a 'period of residential or "block" attendance (e.g. weekend school)' had significantly lower wastage rates than those who had not.

Other factors

There was some tendency for wastage rates to increase as Open University courses got older. For the CNAA courses, the reverse was the case. Wastage seems to be a particularly severe problem during the early years of the life of a course.

In general, the more TV programmes associated with an Open University course, the lower was the wastage rate. This is worth mentioning, as TV programmes are probably the nearest thing (other than summer schools) to face-to-face tuition for Open University students. And it is the availability of face-to-face tuition that is the most important distinguishing feature of CNAA part-time degree courses according to most of the respondents to the CNAA survey.

There was a general tendency for Open University wastage rates to increase with workload. If workload is measured on CNAA part-time degree courses by hours of class attendance plus hours of private study, then no systematic relationship with student non-completion could be found.

Stated reasons for withdrawals

Respondents to the follow-up questionnaire (sent to the CNAA part-time students to track their subsequent progress) who answered that they had withdrawn from their course without any form of award were asked to give the main reason for their withdrawal and any other contributory factors. Only 55 per cent of the non-completers returned the questionnaire (the information on the remaining 45 per cent being obtained from course leaders) so, at best, the information was incomplete. Further, many of those who had withdrawn and returned the questionnaire did not answer the questions on reasons for withdrawal. Recalling the strictures of Woodley and Parlett (1983) on the limited usefulness of information gained from this sort of exercise (response bias, rationalizations and reporting only the *proximate* reason in the multi-causal decision to withdraw), it is unlikely that much of value could, in any case, have been obtained. For these reasons, the following selection of reasons does not claim to be representative and is provided only to illustrate the range of stated reasons for withdrawing.

It is, however, worth noting that of those that did give reasons for withdrawing, a substantial proportion reported that they had transferred to a full-time version of their course. A further fairly large group said that they had withdrawn only temporarily and many of the reasons such as ill-health, work commitments, family responsibilities, and financial problems are included below.

I was offered a different course [which] I preferred and [had] originally applied for.   (Male)

Work commitments required withdrawal from the course. Although [I] intend to complete the course as soon as work allows.   (Female)

[Requesting leave for one year] due to spinal injury.   (Female)

I have taken a year out of the course. I gave birth to a child in November.   (Female)

I have withdrawn for one year. Family responsibilities.   (Female)

Moved with my company from Edinburgh to London. I intended to recommence my studies this year.   (Male)

I have taken one year off to undertake other studies. [Diploma in Applied Social Studies – leading to C.Q.S.W.]   (Female)

Dislike of teaching methods (i.e. long lectures and attendance at necessary times).   (Female)

I am having a year off to do [a full-time conversion course].   (Female)

Due to pressure of work – temporarily withdrawn.   (Male)

I have had a year's break due to raising a family.   (Female)

I had to go into hospital for a disk removal. My employers and the college are happy for myself to complete course when fit.   (Male)

I have had to leave temporarily due to business commitments. Business commitments have prevented me from attending lectures.   (Male)

Completed one year of the course – have now deferred completion for two years because of overseas posting in Middle East.   (Male)

I have taken a year off to retake exams in 1986.   (Female)

Work was becoming more demanding on my time, thus I found I had less time to study. Also I had some other financial priorities.   (Male)

Moving home to take up an appointment in Kent. As I hold two credits with the O.U. I decided to revert back to the O.U. to complete my degree.   (Female)

Although I have failed certain exams thus requiring me to leave the course, I had no intention of continuing with the course even if I had passed. . . . The standard of lecturing left a lot to be desired. . . . On the whole, the course seemed disorganised and ill-prepared.   (Male)

My reason for doing the part-time LLB was because I could not get a grant for [the] first year. I am now receiving a grant.   (Female – transferred into second year of full-time course)

I decided to terminate my employment because my studies were suffering.   (Female – transferred to final-year of full-time course)

I found it too much working full-time, looking after my family as a single parent and studying as well.   (Female – transferred to full-time course with a grant)

Not surprisingly, these responses encompass those who were dissatisfied with various aspects of their courses and those with personal, employment and domestic reasons for withdrawing.

In view of the difficulties with drawing valid conclusions from these responses, a preferable approach is to compare the characteristics of those who had failed to complete with those who continued to make progress towards completion. The results of this exercise are reported in the next section.

Factors associated with non-completion

Research on the causes of non-completion using questionnaire methods has been bedevilled by low response rates (giving much scope for response bias) and suspicions of *ex post facto* rationalizations of the reasons given by the respondents for withdrawal. The method employed in this study sought to overcome these problems by tracking the progress of the students who completed the original questionnaire. This questionnaire produced findings on a wealth of course and student characteristics that could then be cross-tabulated against subsequent non-completion.

We decided to concentrate on the non-completion rates of the 1033 first-year students among the respondents. The reasons for this were:

1. We have shown that non-completion is much higher for students undertaking the first year of their course than for students completing their second and subsequent years. The analysis thus concentrates on that part of courses where the scope for reducing student wastage is greatest.
2. Where a factor is correlated with the distribution of first-year students in the data, there is a danger of erroneously ascribing to the factor an impact on non-completion that, in reality, results from the relative incidence of first-year students in the survey. This is because the non-completion rates are so much higher for first-year students. The danger is removed by restricting attention to first-year students alone.

This section is based on an analysis of the non-completion rates of those first-year respondents who had identified each of the variables in the questionnaire as applying to themselves. It does not distinguish between withdrawals and failures, as this distinction is not as straightforward as it may appear. Students who find the academic level of the course difficult to cope with are likely to withdraw. Students who believe that they will probably fail for any other reason are also likely to withdraw. From this perspective, and also for the purpose of predicting student numbers on subsequent years of the courses, it is better to include all forms of non-completion together.

Where variables are likely to be correlated with each other, care needs to be taken in interpreting the results. Readers can make their own judgements about possible interactions between the factors, although this is picked up in some of the comments on the findings.

Only those results that are statistically significant at the 5 per cent level are reported. Where the number of students is small (less than 100), the percentage figures for non-completion are accompanied by an asterisk. The reason for this is that percentages become less reliable as the population at risk becomes smaller, because atypical results by a few students can more easily distort the results.

In reading the results, it should be borne in mind that the overall non-completion rate for the respondents in the first year of their courses was *26 per cent.*

High student drop-out

First-year non-completion rates were *higher than average* for the following groups of students:

1. *Those who had already considered leaving the course* (non-completion = 47 per cent).

   This apparently simple finding has potentially important implications. A simple question put to students currently enrolled on a course (perhaps halfway through each academic year) asking them whether they have considered leaving the course would identify those who are most at risk from non-completion. Counselling could then be offered to such students. This suggestion would also provide feedback from students on elements of the course that are causing them problems. It seems to have significant advantages over the more common practice of seeking the reasons for student withdrawal *after* they have left.

2. *Those attending on the basis of evenings only* (non-completion = 31 per cent).

   These students presumably received less employer support and experienced greater difficulty in finding the additional time to study. By way of contrast, the non-completion rate of those first-year respondents undertaking courses with a pattern of attendance based on one day each week or one half-day plus evenings was only 14 per cent.

3. *Those for whom the course had generally failed to live up to their expectations when they decided to enrol* (non-completion = 39 per cent*) and *those who would be unwilling to recommend the course to a friend in a similar position to themselves when they started* (non-completion = 49 per cent*).

   Although the numbers of students in these groups are relatively small, this is a clear illustration of non-completion resulting from general dissatisfaction with the course. Dissatisfaction with the following specific factors was associated with higher than average rates of non-completion:

   - relationships between staff and students (non-completion = 48 per cent*);
   - library loan regulations (non-completion = 41 per cent*);
   - refectory/canteen facilities (non-completion = 37 per cent);
   - appreciation by staff of difficulties of part-time study (non-completion = 36 per cent).

4. *Those who regarded the course information that they received before starting the course as 'fairly poor' or 'very poor'* (non-completion = 35 per cent).

   Non-completion rates were particularly high for those who were most dissatisfied with the pre-course information that they received on the *structure* and *content* of the course.

5. *Those for whom the level of course fees was an important factor in the choice of course/institution* (non-completion = 34 per cent).

   An important result of this study is that for the majority of respondents, the level of course fees did not present a problem. However, where course fees are a problem, it is significantly related to non-completion. This lends support to Woodley's (1987) contention that the sudden increase in the number of student drop-outs at the Open University which occurred in 1981 was 'almost certainly a consequence of the large increase in student fees'. It will be seen that this issue recurs in various forms in some subsequent factors.

6. *Those for whom the financial costs of the course caused 'severe hardship' or who found it 'quite difficult to meet the costs'* (non-completion = 35 per cent).
This factor is another reflection of the fact that for the minority for whom fees are a problem it is likely to have a significant effect on their likelihood of completion. By contrast, those who regarded the financial cost as 'not being important' as a barrier to access to part-time degree courses had a non-completion rate of only 21 per cent, and those who responded that the costs of the course were 'no problem at all' had a non-completion rate of only 20 per cent.

7. *Those for whom the required pattern of attendance necessitated more than three journeys to college each week to attend classes* (non-completion = 40 per cent*).
At the other end of the range, those who had to make only one journey to college to attend classes had a lower than average non-completion rate of 21 per cent.

8. *Those on courses which provided for an intermediate qualification and who regarded this as 'very important'* (non-completion = 35 per cent).
These students presumably valued the provision of an intermediate award because they had some doubts about completing the full degree pro-gramme. Those who regarded the presence or absence of an intermediate award as 'unimportant' had a non-completion rate of 19 per cent. This latter group of respondents presumably included a disproportionately large share of those who were confident that their abilities or personal circum-stances were such that they would successfully complete the course, and also a disproportionately large share of those whose ambitions were sharply focused on securing a degree level qualification.

9. *Those who were favourably disposed towards the idea of replacing one session of evening attendance by an equivalent period of attendance on Saturday mornings* (non-completion = 34 per cent).
This finding presumably reflects the fact that a disproportionate number of those who would prefer Saturday morning attendance were finding some evening attendance difficult or inconvenient. Such replacement could, however, generate higher than average non-completion among those for whom Saturday morning classes are difficult or inconvenient.

10. *Those who answered 'Definitely' to the question 'If it were possible for you to complete one or more units by distance learning (i.e. without class attendance) would you be interested in doing this?'* (non-completion = 37 per cent).
The group of students who favoured the introduction of some distance learning units probably contained a high proportion of those who found attending college for classes most difficult or inconvenient.

11. *Those who regarded 'Lack of provision by colleges of preparatory back-to-study' courses*

as a 'Very important' barrier to access to part-time degree courses (non-completion = 34 per cent).

If there is a suggestion that students were projecting their *own* difficulties and needs in this response, then this finding might be interpreted as arguing for more access courses and greater attention to study skills at the start of part-time degree courses.

12. *Those for whom the ability to join the course despite a 'Lack of qualifications' was an important factor in the choice of course/institution* (non-completion = 39 per cent).

The price of a very liberal entry policy is likely to be high student drop-out in the first year of the course. Many course tutors will regard this as a price worth paying. This finding emphasizes the need for finding ways of assessing prior experiential and uncertificated learning. Other aspects of the relationship between level of qualifications and non-completion are picked up later in this chapter.

13. *Those who had no previous experience of* part-time *education* (non-completion = 33 per cent).

Such students encounter not only the problems of induction into the course and the college, but also those of induction into the rigours of part-time study. It would appear that this is often underestimated by those who are new to part-time study and should be emphasized before students make the commitment to enrol.

14. *Those whose highest educational qualification gained* while at school *was below GCE 'O' level standard* (non-completion = 36 per cent).

15. *Those whose highest educational qualification at enrolment was below GCE 'A' level standard* (non-completion = 45 per cent*).

The obvious interpretation of this result is that those with low entry qualifications are likely to encounter greater intellectual difficulties with the academic level of the courses. Other explanations, however, are possible. Part-time undergraduates with low entry qualifications are more likely to be enrolled on evening-only courses, more likely to be in low-income brackets and less likely to receive encouragement and financial assistance from employers. Also, the danger of jumping to the conclusion that there is a simple inverse relationship between entry qualifications and non-completion is apparent from the following finding.

16. *Those who completed their full-time education at age 21+* (non-completion = 35 per cent).

Most of this group already held a degree or postgraduate qualification at the time that they enrolled. It is possible that the motivation to complete was weaker for these students who were presumably more interested in subject knowledge than a high-level qualification. This group may also have contained a relatively high proportion of those whose needs could be met by completing only parts of a course and for whom an associate student scheme would have been more appropriate.

17. *Those who reported that the level of the qualification was 'unimportant' in terms of their choice of course/institution* (non-completion = 44 per cent*).

This group would presumably have a relatively high propensity to leave the course after they had obtained the specific knowledge, understanding or expertise that they joined the course to obtain. An associate student scheme might be more appropriate to the needs of these students.

18. *Those engaged in manual occupations* (non-completion = 35 per cent).
19. *Those who were unemployed* (non-completion = 53 per cent*).
20. *Those who had had at least one spell of unemployment since starting their course* (non-completion = 44 per cent*).
21. *Those who had had more than one spell of unemployment in the 5 years before enrolling on their course* (non-completion = 41 per cent*).
22. *Those whose level of gross personal income in 1985–6 was less than £7000* (non-completion = 30 per cent).
    For those whose gross personal income was over £7000, the non-completion rate was 23 per cent. This is another of the findings that illustrates the importance of the student's financial situation in the decision to leave a course. It is underlined by the following finding.
23. *Those whose level of gross family income in 1985–6 was less than £7000* (non-completion = 46 per cent*).
    By contrast, those whose gross family income in 1985–86 was over £7000, the non-completion rate was only 22 per cent.
24. *Those for whom the course was entirely self-financed* (non-completion = 31 per cent).
    The non-completion rate for those receiving some form of financial assistance with the costs of the course was only 22 per cent. The non-completion rate was particularly low (19 per cent) for those who got financial assistance from a public sector employer.
25. *Those whose average weekly travel time to/from college per week was 6 hours or more* (non-completion = 44 per cent*).
26. *Those whose normal mode of transport to college is other than a car* (non-completion = 33 per cent).
    This might reflect the greater flexibility and convenience of travel by car compared to, say, public transport, or it may reflect the fact that the group that did not travel by car contained a disproportionately high number of less affluent students.
27. *Those who are not married (i.e. single, separated, divorced or widowed)* (non-completion = 30 per cent).
    The non-completion rate for married students was 23 per cent.
28. *Those who considered a CNAA part-time degree to be of a lower standard than a CNAA full-time degree* (non-completion = 37 per cent*), and *those who thought that academics in institutions of higher education considered that a CNAA part-time degree to be of lower standard than a CNAA full-time degree* (non-completion = 32 per cent).
    This finding clearly argues for ensuring that it is made clear to first-year students that the standard of their part-time degree course is equivalent in standard to a CNAA full-time degree course.
29. *Those for whom the difficulties overall were greater than expected when they decided to enrol* (non-completion = 43 per cent).

Those that identified the following factors as giving rise to greater difficulties than expected had significantly higher rates of non-completion:

- coping with the stress of examinations (non-completion = 37 per cent);
- coping with the financial costs of the course (non-completion = 35 per
  cent);
- coping with travel to and from college (non-completion = 35 per cent);
- organizing time in an efficient way (non-completion = 32 per
  cent);
- keeping up with the academic level of the course (non-completion = 32
  per cent);
- coping with job demands (non-completion = 31 per cent).

Some of these factors (such as coping with the stress of examinations and
organizing time in an efficient way) could be addressed within a study skills
component of a part-time degree course. Some could be addressed on an
induction programme that focuses on the difficulties that the students are
likely to encounter. For others, counselling would appear to be the most
effective approach.

30. *Those who had changed their address at least once while on the course* (non-completion
    = 43 per cent*).

    It would seem that moving home can have a very disruptive impact on a
    student's part-time studies.

31. *Those who reported their main aim when enrolling to be to 'Increase the opportunities for
    changing my job'* (non-completion = 37 per cent*).

32. *Those who identified the following changes in their circumstances as having increased
    their difficulties in pursuing their course:*

- change of employer (non-completion = 48 per cent*);
- change in state of health (non-completion = 48 per cent*).

33. *Those who had missed at least 5 per cent of their classes to date due to work commitments*
    (non-completion = 43 per cent).

34. *Those who reported that they had been unable to complete required reading or course work
    because of work commitments* (non-completion = 32 per cent).

35. *Those who had missed classes due to domestic commitments* (non-completion =
    43 per cent*).

36. *Those who expressed a preference for 'more formal lectures and less of other forms of class
    contact'* (non-completion = 35 per cent).

    It may be that these students are more dependent and less able to take
    responsibility for their own learning than those who placed less value on
    lectures. Alternatively, it may simply be that these are the students with the
    greatest pressures on their time.

37. *Those who expressed a preference for 'More class attendance and less private study'*
    (non-completion = 33 per cent*).

    This finding prompts similar comments to those made about the previous
    factor. Possibly, this group contains a higher than average proportion of
    those who would prefer more of a 'spoonfed' approach than is commonly

found on degree courses. This raises a possible conflict between meeting the self-perceived needs of the students and maintaining the standards of the course in terms of academic process.

Low student drop-out

First-year non-completion rates were *lower than average* for the following groups of students:

1. *Those who first heard about their course from someone currently (or previously) enrolled on the course* (non-completion = 18 per cent).
    Such students are likely to benefit from discussion with those who have first-hand experience of the course. This can be an especially effective way of communicating information that is difficult to convey in other ways (such as the relationships between staff and students). Also, of course, current and past students are only likely to recommend courses that have given a high level of satisfaction.
2. *Those who attached importance in their choice of course/institution to the fact that 'Spouse/friends etc. were already taking this course'* (non-completion = 15 per cent).
    This finding emphasizes the potential role of current (and past) students as agents of recruitment. It also emphasizes the importance of developing social cohesiveness among the students enrolled on a course.
3. *Those who enrolled on a CNAA part-time degree course rather than an Open University course because they believed that the 'CNAA course had a better reputation/recommended'* (non-completion = 21 per cent).
    This finding again emphasizes the value of existing and past students in the recruitment process and of informal channels of recruitment in general.
4. *Those who first heard about their course from their employer* (non-completion = 18 per cent).
    Apparently, courses that direct their advertising at local employers are likely to have lower non-completion than other courses. In this case, the students are more likely to get some release from work to attend their course and other forms of employer support.
5. *Those who had attended a period of residential or 'block' release, (e.g. weekend school)* (non-completion = 19 per cent). This result confirms the recommendation made earlier in this book that course teams consider the merits of including a weekend residential at an early stage in part-time degree courses. It parallels the finding of Woodley and Parlett (1983) that Open University students who had attended a summer school were less likely to drop out.
6. *Those who expressed a high level of satisfaction with the following factors*:
    *   availability in library of books and journals recommended by staff (non-completion = 21 per cent);
    *   library loan regulations (non-completion = 21 per cent);
    *   appreciation by staff of the difficulties of part-time study (non-completion = 22 per cent).

7. *Those who had found independent work, e.g. project work, particularly helpful* (non-completion = 20 per cent).
   This is perhaps a good reason for including the issue of independent work in the development of appropriate study skills.

8. *Those who had studied at the same college before* (non-completion = 19 per cent).
   New students are likely to encounter problems of adjustment to the college and the course. Students who had studied at the college before would be familiar with the college environment and college facilities (and possibly also the course), so that problems of adjustment to the college would be absent. The non-completion rate for respondents who had not studied at the same college before was 10 per cent higher at 29 per cent.

9. *Those who rated the following objectives in enrolling for their course as 'very important':*

   • to make new friends with similar interests (non-completion = 14 per cent*);
   • to improve my chances of promotion/increased salary in my present type of work (non-completion = 18 per cent);
   • to help me do my present job better (non-completion = 16 per cent);
   • to prove to myself (or others) that I could complete a degree course (non-completion = 22 per cent).

10. *Those who had known about the existence of their course for 2 years or more before enrolling* (non-completion = 21 per cent).
    Most of these students had not enrolled earlier because they lacked the necessary educational qualifications or because of work or domestic commitments. They appear to be students who had made serious efforts to get themselves prepared for their course in terms of other commitments or educational prerequisites. As such, they probably represent a group with high motivation and who are unwilling to commit themselves impulsively.

11. *Those whose entry qualification was a teaching certificate or diploma* (non-completion = 13 per cent).
    Typically, these students were enrolled on courses in education of relatively short duration that did not involve evening-only attendance and they had the support of their employers.

12. *Those whose entry qualification was an HNC/HND* (non-completion = 21 per cent).
    Typically, these students were enrolled on courses of relatively short duration that did not involve evening-only attendance and they had the support of their employers. Also, most of these students held an HNC – a qualification normally obtained on the basis of previous *part-time* study.

13. *Those married students with spouses who had undertaken courses of part-time education* (non-completion = 19 per cent).
    Presumably, these students would be from home environments where the difficulties of undertaking part-time study are appreciated. They are therefore likely to have particularly supportive home backgrounds.

14. *Those respondents employed as teachers* (non-completion = 12 per cent).
    Because most of these students held a teaching certificate or diploma as an

entry qualification and were enrolled on the relatively short courses in education, this factor is clearly correlated with other factors associated with low rates of non-completion.

15. *Those respondents employed as technical personnel, including data processing, draughts-men and technicians* (non-completion = 19 per cent).

    Again, there are problems of interpretation with this factor, as a high proportion of these students held HNC qualifications and were enrolled on relatively short courses in engineering/technology with time for course attendance made available by their employers.

16. *Those employed by a public sector authority* (non-completion = 21 per cent).

    It is difficult to know whether this is a general result or simply reflects the fact that this group contains a large group of teachers whose rate of non-completion is particularly low.

17. *Those who reported that encouragement by their employer was an important factor in the choice of course/institution* (non-completion = 18 per cent).

18. *Those respondents in employment who had been employed with their current employer for at least 3 years* (non-completion = 22 per cent).

    This compares with a non-completion rate of 31 per cent for those who had completed less than 3 years with their current employer.

19. *Those for whom the following people were seen as being 'very supportive'*:
    - fellow students (non-completion = 21 per cent);
    - college staff (non-completion = 21 per cent);
    - spouse/partner (non-completion = 22 per cent);
    - employer (non-completion = 22 per cent).

20. *Those receiving tangible employer support of the following kinds*:

    - employer pays or refunds all of the course fees (non-completion = 19 per cent);
    - employer makes an allowance for travelling (non-completion = 16 per cent);
    - employer gives time off with pay to attend classes (non-completion = 21 per cent).

21. *Those who envisaged undertaking further study after completing their present degree course*:

    - postgraduate research degree (non-completion = 18 per cent);
    - taught master's course (non-completion = 19 per cent);
    - professional updating course (non-completion = 19 per cent).

Summary

This chapter is based on an analysis of the subsequent progress of those students who had completed the initial questionnaire. One year after the original questionnaire, almost two-thirds of the respondents were still enrolled and over one-fifth had successfully completed their courses. Three per cent had failed and 1 per cent had left with an intermediate award.

1. *Non-completion as performance indicator.* Non-completion is very important, but as a general performance indicator it is a blunt instrument. It can encourage some practices that are commendable but it can also encourage undesirable practices. High rates of non-completion usually produce difficulties for those administering part-time degree courses (particularly at the advanced stages) and this itself is a discipline. The evidence from the course leaders' questionnaire showed a high level of awareness of the problem of non-completion. Part-time degree course with high rates of non-completion probably need help rather than censure.

2. *Non-completion as a function of years completed.* The non-completion rate was much higher for the respondents in the first year of their courses than for those in subsequent years. In general, the more years that students had been enrolled, the smaller the proportion that withdrew without any form of award.

3. *Non-completion as a function of length of course.* The level of non-completion is much higher for students on longer courses (4 years or more) than for shorter courses (3 years or less).

4. *Non-completion as a function of the age of the course.* Non-completion rates are likely to be particularly high during the early life of a course. It is at this stage that course team needs the greatest support and assistance in dealing with the problem of non-completion.

5. *Comparison with Open University.* Compared with the Open University, student non-completion rates are higher in the first year of CNAA undergraduate programmes but, for subsequent years, the rate of non-completion is higher for the Open University students. It appears that those who enrol on CNAA part-time degree courses experience the difficulty of adjustment when they first enrol on their course, and that this is more severe (or they are less well-prepared for it) than that experienced by new Open University undergraduates. However, it also seems that this adjustment occurs only at the start of the CNAA courses, whereas it recurs for the Open University students with each additional course that they take.

6. *Correlates of student non-completion.* The final part of the chapter identifies a wide range of variables associated with first-year non-completion. Some of these may be termed 'course-orientated', as they primarily reflect factors that relate to the structure or practices of courses (or colleges). Some are 'student-orientated', as they primarily reflect characteristics of the students that are identifiable at enrolment. The remainder reflect, for the most part, the experience of students since enrolment.

   On the evidence of this survey, the simplest solution to the problem of non-completion is to recruit only applicants in the 'low-risk' categories, but this would undermine the aspirations for increased access to higher education that prompted the development of most part-time degree courses.

7. *Counselling approach.* A more acceptable approach would be to place more

emphasis on pre-enrolment counselling of applicants in the 'high-risk' categories identified above. In addition, counselling *all* applicants about the factors (identified above) that increase the risks of non-completion would clearly be helpful.

8. *Course review.* The findings reported in this chapter should be useful in suggesting modifications to particular courses that can be helpful in reducing non-completion.

It seems likely that non-completion is often underestimated when courses are first developed and that the experience with running courses leads to small changes that effect gradual reductions in the context of specific courses. Some of these are implicit in the findings presented in this chapter and form the basis for some of the recommendations in Chapter 9.

9 | Conclusions, Implications and Recommendations

Part-time degree courses are a significant national asset. Until the mid-1980s, their growth had received little recognition. More recently, the tide has begun to turn in their favour as part of the growing interest in the development of policy towards continuing education.

In this last chapter, we have resisted the temptation to enter the broad debate on continuing education. Our focus throughout this book has been on part-time degree courses and the experience of the students who enrol on them. We have tried to maintain that focus in this chapter by concentrating on the practical implications of our research findings at the level of the colleges, the management of the courses and the students.

Conclusions and recommendations

Publicity and recruitment

The scale of part-time degree course provision nationally within the polytechnics and colleges sector of higher education has now reached a level where there is a prima facie case for some central initiative in disseminating information. This would not, of course, eliminate the need for local recruitment efforts at course level, but it would probably have a significant impact on the effectiveness of those efforts. Relatively low student enrolment on many part-time degree courses suggests that more concerted advertising of these courses would produce more efficient utilization of the resources that are committed to them.

About 90 per cent of the respondents to the students' questionnaire said 'yes' to the question 'Would you recommend this course to a friend in a similar position to yourself when you started?' Courses with low levels of recruitment should bear this finding in mind. The existing students and graduates are potentially powerful agents of recruitment. Course teams might also consider whether greater awareness of part-time degree course opportunities within smaller organizations would be worth pursuing.

About 30 per cent of the students reported that they are members of a professional body. Most professional bodies have an interest in education and they offer a potentially cost-effective medium through which to make contact with potential students.

Access courses and associate student schemes

Mounting an access course and securing an interface with an institution of higher education is a much more daunting task than developing and operating an associate student scheme. The findings of the research project indicates that an associate student scheme can be used in combination with an institution's part-time degree courses to strengthen this route into higher education.

Admissions

Our findings on entry qualifications of CNAA part-time undergraduates suggest that, overall, admissions tutors may be unduly conservative in their admissions policies. Some courses might consider the value of tests combined with less demanding requirements in terms of conventional entry qualifications. Until effective methods of evaluating experiential learning have been identified and disseminated to admissions tutors, this could provide a more flexible admissions policy while still preserving the security required by many courses.

Even when courses are enabled to make more use of the opportunities to enrol students with non-standard entry qualifications and, in particular, to give credit for experiential learning (see Evans, 1984) in entry criteria, there will still be a need to provide greater awareness of this to potential students.

Application forms

The key criterion for any application form is: Is it likely to encourage applicants to present themselves as well as possible and also provide a basis for an informed decision about the applicant? Candidates should be encouraged to identify their accomplishments (whether at work or elsewhere) and outline their aspirations for themselves. It is undesirable to ask part-time applicants to complete application forms designed for younger applicants of full-time courses. There would appear to be much merit in an institution producing its own 'core' application form for use across all its part-time courses. Individual courses can then append a sheet asking for any further information that is required for the specific needs of the course.

Admissions interviews

Approximately 70 per cent of the survey's respondents attended an interview for their course. An admissions interview can take the form of educational counselling in which the needs of the applicant are explored to assess whether the course is the most appropriate one to meet those needs. This is clearly most important for those applicants in the 'high risk' categories identified in Chapter 8. An interview that included admissions counselling of this kind would seem to be one means of reducing unnecessary non-completion by students. In view of this, it may seem surprising that almost 30 per cent of our respondents attended no interview and it is difficult to resist the feeling that some courses are losing an opportunity here.

Almost 40 per cent of the respondents claim not to have considered an Open University course when they applied for their CNAA part-time degree course. This is a disturbingly high figure and one might have hoped that all applicants to CNAA part-time degree courses (and to applicants to part-time courses of the universities including the Open University) would be encouraged to consider the alternatives in order to identify the course of higher education that most meets their needs. An admissions interview is an appropriate place for this sort of educational counselling.

Interviews are often used for imparting information to candidates as well as assessing the suitability of a candidate for a place on a course. The information is usually imparted orally some time before admission to a course and the students are interacting with the institution in the role of applicant. It might be helpful to distinguish between information that the applicant needs to assist in the decision about whether to accept an offer of a place on a course and that which might be more accurately described as induction information. The latter type of information is best conveyed outside of admissions interviews. Some courses arrange for additional interactions with groups of new students where information about the course and institution is made available. Other courses might like to consider this approach.

Information for new students

It is easier to provide information to students on some matters than on others. Informing students of the amount of required class attendance is not difficult. Providing information on the level of academic difficulty of a course is much less easy. It should, however, be possible to give students a reasonable appreciation of the teaching methods that they can expect and it should be possible in an interview situation to provide a fair indication of the amount of required private study. In fact, this is just the sort of information that is best conveyed in an interview.

The development of a 'core' document of information for part-time students by an institution to which individual courses can append departmental and course specific information might be considered as an effective means of providing institutional and course information while offering resource savings to the institution.

Student awareness of likely difficulties

The admissions interview would also seem to be an appropriate vehicle for exploring with the prospective student likely difficulties. Certainly, it would seem to be important – at some stage in the admissions process – for staff to emphasize to students the difficulties that they are likely to encounter.

Over 50 per cent of the students surveyed encountered more difficulty finding the time to study than they had expected when they enrolled. Almost 40 per cent perceived this a problem of time management. For others it may be a question of being made more aware of the required level of weekly time commitment needed to complete the course and being encouraged to work carefully through their priorities to discover where the time can be found. An admissions interview would seem to be an appropriate place to start this process and it would seem sensible to spend some time of any induction programme addressing this issue.

Difficulties associated with domestic commitments were often greater than expected for part-time students, and applicants should be encouraged at an early stage to discuss the level of commitment necessary to complete a part-time degree level course with their family to ensure that this really is appreciated.

An important factor impacting on non-completion was financial difficulties. Hopefully, the information in this book (especially Chapter 6) will prove useful to those involved in the admissions process in helping applicants to appreciate realistically the likely financial impact of undertaking part-time undergraduate studies.

Study skills

Helping students to learn how to learn is an important objective for courses of education at all levels. Facts become outdated, but learning how to learn more effectively benefits students for the rest of their lives. The development of study skills is one significant element of this.

For those without any experience of study since their last full-time course, insecurity about 'rusty' study skills is a significant problem. Developing appropriate study skills and coping with the stress of examinations each proved more difficult than expected for more than 20 per cent of the respondents. There does seem to be a strong case for explicitly addressing the issue of study skills at the outset of part-time degree courses.

At least one course known to the authors starts with a residential weekend for new students orientated towards developing study skills. This residential also, of course, helps to develop social cohesiveness among the students with its additional educational benefits. Course teams might consider this as an example of good practice.

Sometimes the development of study skills is under the direction of the library staff or the institution's educational development service. These central services are unlikely to provide sufficient service by themselves: the study skills required of students vary across subjects and in relation to the course objectives.

Some staff involved in operating part-time degree courses may, as subject specialists, not feel confident about facilitating study skills workshops. Where this is the case, they might consider using available videos that address these issues and they might also consider what help can be sought within their institution from their own educational development units, counselling services or departments of education.

Course flexibility

One factor that afforded least satisfaction to the students in the survey was the opportunity to vary the pace of their studies. Course structures that are flexible in this way, however, tend to be more resource-intensive than simple but inflexible structures, and this is presumably one reason for the observed lack of flexibility of many of the courses. Nevertheless, course teams could usefully direct their attention to ways of permitting students to vary the pace of their studies.

Course transfers

Because, at most institutions, part-time degree courses exist alongside corresponding full-time degree courses, arrangements could be made to facilitate transfers from the latter to the former. This may require better communication between the two modes than exists at present in some colleges.

Intermediate awards

Considerable difficulties confront the student in sustaining high-level study over the necessarily long duration of a part-time degree course. Domestic and professional circumstances can change in unpredictable ways, so that the probability of successful completion cannot be so high as for full-time students. For this reason, it is desirable that part-time students perceive objectives that are realistically attainable in their not-too-distant futures. Moreover, it is also desirable to make provisions that allow for the students to adjust their objectives as the course progresses.

Some potential students are unsure of their capacity to complete a full degree course. Such students are likely to draw confidence from the presence of an intermediate award for the successful completion of the initial stages of the degree course. On the evidence of our survey, the large majority of part-time undergraduates favour the availability of an intermediate award.

The impact of intermediate certification on student numbers is unclear. It is likely to increase enrolments but, in so far as some students will leave with the intermediate award, it is also likely to increase non-completion. It is difficult to see, however, how it could not be in the students' interests. In view of this, and as it is not difficult to introduce, it is recommended for the consideration of courses and colleges.

Intensive teaching

There is evidence from the survey of part-time students concurrently studying what appears to be an unreasonably large number of different subjects. Would it not be better, in some cases, to teach subjects in series rather than in parallel? For example, instead of teaching four subjects in parallel over a whole year, perhaps it would be worth considering the desirability of teaching two subjects more intensively for one semester each. By reducing the range of subjects with which the student must cope at any one time, workloads would be made more manageable, examinations would be staggered thereby reducing the amplitude of examination pressures, and it would also provide more entry points to the course – permitting more flexibility for exemptions. There have been some experiments with 'intensive teaching' (see, for example, Parlett and King, 1971), and part-time degree courses could be a fruitful field in which to apply the results.

Coursework

Coursework accounts, on average, for about 30 per cent of the assessment within CNAA part-time degree courses. Only 5 per cent of the respondents wanted it to have a smaller role in assessment than it currently does on their courses. On the evidence of this study, course teams that wish to increase the proportion of assessment accounted for by coursework would encounter little resistance from the students.

Distance learning

The findings from this research project suggest that there is scope for introducing some *optional* distance learning units into CNAA part-time degree courses and that this would have a favourable effect on student retention. Some of the students, at least, would appreciate greater freedom to choose. However, the findings also suggest the scope for fundamental innovations in this area is not great.

Programmed learning

Few of the survey's respondents reported that they found programmed learning either pleasant or helpful. It would appear that distance learning based on programmed instruction would not find much support among these students.

Social cohesion

About 60 per cent of the respondents said that more contact with tutors and fellow students was a reason for choosing a CNAA part-time degree course rather than an Open University course. There would appear to be an important social dimension to the educational experience of those who choose CNAA part-time degree courses. Those who are responsible for operating part-time degree courses might wish to reflect on how this can be developed to enhance the learning experience and the likelihood of successful completion.

Residentials

Residentials offer an opportunity to make available to the students a wider range of study methods and learning activities and to develop social cohesiveness among the course members. Our research indicates that they also reduce the likelihood of non-completion. In the light of our findings, a weekend residential orientated towards enhancing study skills, improved time management and the development of self-help groups would be worth considering as a way of starting most part-time degree courses.

Student feedback

Two dimensions of the courses which afforded least satisfaction to the students in the survey were the feedback to students on their performance and arrangements for them to make their voices heard in course evaluation. Course teams might wish to reflect on ways in which feedback to students on their performance can be improved and ways in which feedback from students can be more systematically incorporated into the course evaluation process. Course management teams might like to compare the level of satisfaction of students on their own courses with the findings of this survey.

Academic support

Non-completion was higher for students who had missed classes due to work commitments or domestic commitments. The practice of providing, at the beginning of each session, a programme of the topics that will be covered each week (with appropriate readings), enables the student who has to miss classes for a week to maintain the continuity of their studies by private study. This practice has much to commend it.

At a more speculative level, it is possible that course providers could make greater use of cassette tapes as a means of tuition. The range of materials on cassette tapes has substantially increased in recent years, and this is a resource that could be investigated. Alternatively, taped lectures would be an innovation which many part-time students might find attractive (see Gibbs *et al.*, 1984).

Counselling

On the evidence of this study, much reliance is placed on central counselling services for counselling part-time students. Institutions might benefit from a review of the adequacy of these counselling facilities. We recommend that there should be a member of the counselling service within each institution with explicit responsibility for ensuring that the counselling needs of part-time students are addressed.

Personal tutors

It is important that students on part-time degree courses recognize some member of staff (whether personal tutor or not) on their course with whom they can discuss difficulties that impact on their studies if only to ensure that the problems are, where appropriate, brought to the attention of the relevant examinations board. On a small part-time degree course, it may be sufficient if the students can discuss problems with the course leader or a year tutor. Ideally, one would wish that some member(s) of each course team would be equipped with counselling skills.

Support from others

The respondents drew most encouragement from their family and other members of the course (staff and fellow students). Course teams might reflect on how students might be encouraged to widen the base of their support to include less obvious people who are influential in their lives such as friends outside of work.

This study has revealed a generally supportive attitude by the employers of part-time undergraduates and that those with this support are less likely to drop out. This raises the question of whether courses could facilitate the manifestation of this supportive attitude by providing students with estimates of some of the costs of completing the course (such as estimates of the cost of books and equipment requirements), and by certifying the reasonableness of items such as travel costs to and from college. This would presumably make it easier for students to claim support and it would probably also make it easier for employers to provide the support.

Courses might wish to consider facilitating the development of self-help groups among the students to provide mutual support for when the going gets difficult.

On-site facilities

For over 50 per cent of the respondents, the availability of on-site facilities (libraries, computers, etc.) was a reason for choosing a CNAA part-time degree course rather than an Open University degree course. College authorities could bear this in mind when they are making decisions about college facilities that will affect part-time students.

Library facilities

The students in this survey expressed good levels of satisfaction with the library opening hours and loan regulations but rather less satisfaction with the *availability* of books and journals recommended by staff. Some libraries make special library loan arrangements for part-time students and libraries might wish to compare practices in this area.

Refectory and pre-school child-care facilities

These were two factors that produced the highest proportions of dissatisfied respondents in the students' questionnaire. In a period of diminishing units of real resource, it is inevitable that there will be an impact on the adequacy of some facilities. However, it would be instructive to compare the ways that different colleges have coped in terms of the impact on part-time students.

Grant regulations

There remains an anomaly within the student grant regulations whereby a student who undertakes part of a part-time degree at his/her own expense becomes, thereby, ineligible for a mandatory award for *completing* the final stage by full-time study.

Fees

Institutions might well consider the precedent of two institutions in this survey by investigating opportunities for introducing a 'payment by instalments' scheme for part-time students.

Students' unions

About two-thirds of the respondents were unaware of belonging to a students' union at their college. We recommend that students' unions review their practices with respect to part-time students.

Fruitful co-existence of part-time courses at different levels

Over 30 per cent of the respondents had experience of previous study at the college at which they were enrolled for their CNAA part-time degree course. Over 20 per cent gave this as a reason for choosing their course rather than an Open University degree course. The maintenance of non-degree part-time courses is likely to be important to healthy enrolments on part-time courses at degree level.

A *majority* of the respondents expressed some positive interest in proceeding to further part-time study for a higher level academic course if this were possible at the college at which they were currently enrolled. This will be good news to those engaged in the development of postgraduate part-time degree courses for whom information on potential demand is difficult to obtain. It emphasizes the value of the fruitful co-existence of part-time courses at different levels within the same institution.

Council for National Academic Awards

The CNAA has produced no policy document focused on part-time students as a whole. In view of the growth in part-time degree course provision over the last decade, it is timely for the CNAA to conduct a general review to ensure that its policies in relation to part-time degree courses in general are co-ordinated at the level of regulations, administrative procedures and in terms of relationships with funding bodies and professional bodies.

Shared experience

Running a part-time course can be an onerous and isolated experience for the staff involved. It would be helpful if mechanisms could be developed to facilitate the sharing of experience among those responsible for the administration of part-time courses. One precedent exists in the Standing Committee for Part-time Degrees in Business Studies. This precedent could usefully be followed in those subject areas with a significant number (five?) of part-time degree courses. This could facilitate the dissemination of best practice, it could facilitate the solution of problems that individual course leaders are ill-equipped to tackle on their own, it could establish identifiable groups with expertise, and it could provide a source of information and help for those who are developing new part-time degree courses.

Further research

Efficiency of the part-time mode

It is very likely that the social cost–benefit balance for part-time degree courses is very favourable (and not reflected in the resources allocated to part-time degree courses nationally as reflected in FTE weighting for part-time students). This is, of course, only the gut feeling of the authors. The following work could make a valuable contribution to efficient and effective resource allocation within higher education:

1. An assessment of the costs of producing a graduate by different modes of attendance.
2. An estimation of the social rate of return of producing a graduate by different modes of attendance.

Awareness of availability of part-time degree courses

The HMI Report on *Part-time Advanced Further Education* (DES, 1985, p. 34) concluded that:

> At present, part-time courses of advanced further education are an under-utilised national resource; the major conclusion of this report is that increased enrolments on many courses could be accommodated at relatively small marginal cost and with advantages for the quality of the education and of the workforce in general.

In 1983, research by Market and Opinion Research International (MORI) for Middlesex Polytechnic revealed highly inaccurate perceptions about awareness of the work of the polytechnics among MPs, 'captains of industry' and the public at large. It would be valuable to discover what awareness there is of the opportunities to study for a part-time degree in the vicinities of the polytechnics, universities and other colleges where part-time courses are available.

Associate student schemes

On the evidence of this project, it would seem that associate or occasional student schemes can provide an effective route into higher education for part-time students. A small but useful exercise would be to map the availability of these schemes across institutions of higher education. It would also be useful to survey and compare the provisions of these schemes so that institutions could identify what, from their own perspective, represents best practice.

Perceptions of the standard of part-time degree courses

Three-quarters of the respondents to our survey thought that their part-time degree courses are of equivalent standard to full-time degree courses. Of the remainder, a majority thought that the part-time degree courses are of a higher standard. However, they were far less confident about the perceptions of others. Overall, they thought that their employers were less inclined to rate the relative standard of their part-time courses as highly as they did themselves and they were even less optimistic about the perceptions of academics in institutions of higher education.

Over 25 per cent of the respondents thought that academics in institutions of higher education believe that part-time degree courses are of a lower standard than full-time degree courses. It would be of interest to discover whether this has any basis in fact. If it does not, then it would clearly be helpful to provide the students with reassurance on this matter. This is especially important in view of the substantial percentage of the respondents who wish to use their part-time degrees as a basis for further academic study.

Admissions counselling

In view of the fact that a substantial proportion of the respondents had not considered an Open University course, then it would also be interesting to know what percentage of Open University students had not considered a CNAA part-time degree (or one at a local university) when making their choice of undergraduate studies.

Credit transfer

Less than 1 per cent of the students who responded to the questionnaire held Open University credits. It would be interesting to know what percentage of Open University students obtain credit on the basis of partial completion of part-time degree courses of the CNAA or the other universities.

On-course counselling

In view of the evidence from this project that much reliance is placed by course leaders on central counselling services, it would be worthwhile to investigate the extent to which part-time undergraduates actually use the central counselling services of the institutions. It would also be worthwhile examining the availability of central counselling services to part-time undergraduates, particularly evening-only students.

Mixed-ability groups

The arts and humanities, and social studies subject groups both have higher than average proportions of students with particularly high qualifications and also higher than average proportions with relatively low entry qualifications. It would be interesting to discover whether this wide variation results in difficulties in teaching the students together.

Part-time postgraduate students

The research project on which this course is based focused on students enrolled on part-time *undergraduate* programmes. A similar project focused on part-time students on *postgraduate* programmes would be worthwhile. It would be particularly valuable to examine the experience of those enrolled on *part-time* postgraduate *research* degrees.

References

Ball, C. (1985). *Fitness for Purpose: Essays in Higher Education by Christopher Ball* (D. Unwin, ed.). SRHE/Windsor: NFER-Nelson.

Bourner, T. (1979). The cost of completing a part-time degree by full-time study. *Higher Education Review*, **12**(1), 55–69.

Bourner, T. (1983). Part-time first degree courses of the Council for National Academic Awards. *Educational Studies*, **19**(1) 17–30.

Bourner, T. and McQueen, W. (1983). The relationships between part-time and sandwich degree courses in business studies. *Business Education*, **4**(1), 3–18.

Department of Education and Science (1974). *Statistics of Education*. Vol. 4, London: DES.

Department of Education and Science (1978). *Higher Education into the 1990s*. London: DES.

Department of Education and Science (1985). *Part-time Advanced Further Education: HMI Survey of Advanced Courses*. London: DES.

Evans, N. (1984). *Access to Higher Education: Non-standard Entry to CNAA First Degree and DipHE Courses*. CNAA Development Services Publication 6. London: CNAA.

Fulton, O., Hamilton, M., Slowey, M., Wagner, L. and Woodley, A (1987). *Choosing to Learn: Adults in Education*. SRHE/Milton Keynes: Open University Press.

Gibbs, G., Habershaw, S. and Habershaw, T. (1984). *53 Interesting Things to do in Your Lectures*. Bristol: Technical and Educational Services Ltd.

NEDC (1984). *Changing Work Patterns and Practices*. London: NEDC.

Parlett, M. and King, J. (1971). *Concentrated Study: A Pedagogic Experiment Observed*. Guildford: SRHE.

Percy, K., Longham, M. and Adams, J. (1982). *Educational Information, Advisory and Counselling Services for Adults: A Sourcebook*. Lancaster Series on Adult Education, No. 3. Lancaster: University of Lancaster.

Phythian, T. and Clements, M. (1982). Drop-out from third level maths courses. *Teaching at a Distance*, **21**, 35–44.

Piper, D. (ed.) (1982). *Is Higher Education Fair?* Guildford: SRHE.

Robbins Report (1963). *Report of the Committee on Higher Education under the Chairmanship of Lord Robbins*. CNMD 2154. London: HMSO.

Robinson, E. (1968). *The New Polytechnics*. Harmondsworth: Penguin.

Rogers, C. (1983). *Freedom to Learn for the 80s*. Merrill, Columbus: Ohio.

Tolley, G. (1975). Address given to a conference of part-time students organized by the National Union of Students.

Turnstall, J. (1974). *The Open University Opens*. London: Routledge.

Wagner, L. and Watts, A. (1976). *The Costs of Being a Student* (mimeo). See also *Times Higher Education Supplement*, 12 November 1976.

Whitburn, J., Mealing, M. and Cox, C. (1976). *People in Polytechnics*. Guildford: SRHE.

Woodley, A. (1987). Understanding adult student drop-out. In *Open Learning for Adults* (D. Grugeson and M. Thorpe, eds). Halow: Longman.

Woodley, A. and McIntosh, N. (1980). *The Door Stood Open – An Evaluation of the Open University Younger Students' Pilot Scheme*. Lewes: Falmer Press.

Woodley, A. and Parlett, M. (1983). Student drop-out. *Teaching at a Distance*, **24**, 2–23.

Index

The Society for Research into Higher Education

The Society exists both to encourage and co-ordinate research and development into all aspects of Higher Education; including academic, organizational and policy issues; and also to provide a forum for debate, verbal and printed.

The Society's income derives from subscriptions, book sales, conference fees, and grants. It receives no subsidies and is wholly independent. Its corporate members are institutions of higher education, research institutions and professional, industrial, and governmental bodies. Its individual members include teachers and researchers, administrators and students. Members are found in all parts of the world and the Society regards its international work as amongst its most important activities.

The Society is opposed to discrimination in higher education on grounds of belief, race, etc.

The Society discusses and comments on policy, organizes conferences, and encourages research. It is studying means of preserving archives of higher education. Under the imprint SRHE & OPEN UNIVERSITY PRESS it is a specialist publisher of research, having some 30 titles in print. The Editorial Board of the Society's Imprint seeks authoritative research or study in the field. It offers competitive royalties; a highly recognizable format in both hard- and paper-back; and the world-wide reputation of the Open University Press. The Society also publishes *Studies in Higher Education* (three times a year), which is mainly concerned with academic issues; *Higher Education Quarterly* (formerly *Universities Quarterly*), mainly concerned with policy issues; *Abstracts* (three times a year); an *International Newsletter* (twice a year) and *S.R.H.E. NEWS* (four times a year).

The Society's Committees, Study Groups and Branches are run by members (with help from a small secretariat at Guildford). The Groups at present include a Teacher Education Study Group, a Staff Development Group, a Continuing Education Group, a Women in Higher Education Group and an Excellence in Teaching Group. The Groups may have their own organization, subscriptions, or publications; (e.g. the *Staff Development Newsletter*). A further *Question of Quality* Group has organized a series of Anglo-American seminars in the USA and the UK.

The Society's annual conferences are held jointly; 'Access & Institutional Change' (1989, with the Polytechnic of North London). In 1990, the topic will be 'Industry and Higher Education' (with the University of Surrey). In 1991, the topic will be 'Research and Higher Education', with the University of Leicester: in 1992, it will be 'Learning and Teaching' (with Nottingham Polytechnic). In 1993, the topic will be 'Governments, Higher Education and Accountability'. Other conferences have considered the 'HE After the Election' (1987) and 'After the Reform Act' (July 1988).

Members receive free of charge the Society's *Abstracts*, annual conference Proceedings, (or 'Precedings'), *S.R.H.E. News* and *International Newsletter*. They may buy *SRHE & Open University Press* books at 35 per cent discount, and *Higher Education Quarterly* on special terms. Corporate members also receive the Society's journal *Studies in Higher Education* free; (individuals on special terms). Members may also obtain certain other journals at a discount, including the NFER *Register of Educational Research*. There is a substantial discount to members, and to staff of corporate members, on annual and some other conference fees. The discounts can exceed the subscription.

		Annual Subscriptions August 1990–July 1991
Individual members		£43.00
Students & retired members		£12.00
Hardship		£20.00
Corporate members		
less than 1000 students		£155.00
1000–3000 students		£195.00
more than 3000 students		£290.00
Non-teaching bodies	up to	£295.00

 *Further information*: SRHE at the University, Guildford GU2 5XH, UK Tel: (0483) 39003 Fax: (0483) 300903
Catalogue: *SRHE & Open University Press*, Celtic Court, 22 Ballmoor, Buckingham MK18 1XW. Tel: (0280) 823388